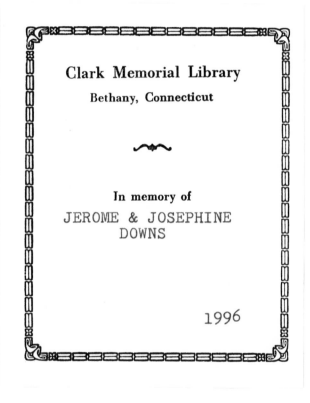

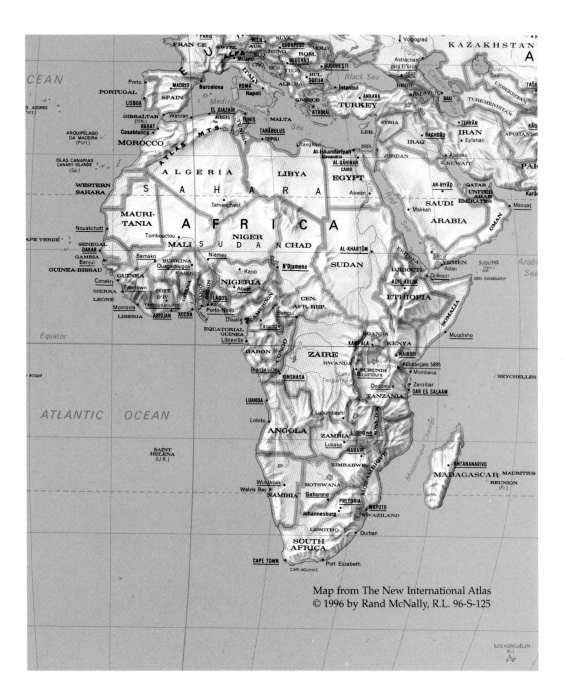

Map from The New International Atlas
© 1996 by Rand McNally, R.L. 96-S-125

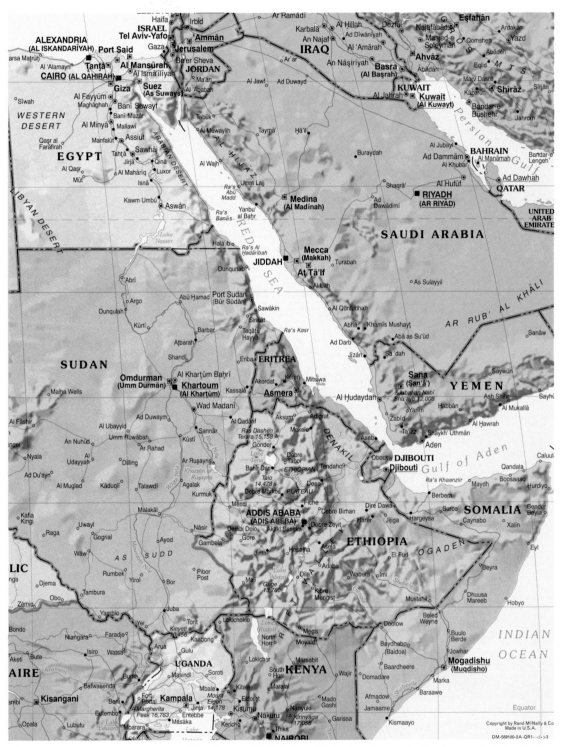

Map from Quick Reference World Atlas © 1996 by Rand McNally, R.L. 96-S-125

Enchantment of the World

SOMALIA

By Mary Virginia Fox

Consultant for Somalia: Robert F. Gorman, Ph.D., Professor of
Political Science, Southwest Texas State University, San Marcos, Texas

CHILDREN'S PRESS®
A Division of Grolier Publishing
New York • London • Hong Kong • Sydney
Danbury, Connecticut

A modern Somali woman walks down a sheltered street in Mogadishu.

Project Editor and Design: Jean Blashfield Black
Photo Research: Jay Mallin

Library of Congress Cataloging-in-Publication Data

Fox, Mary Virginia.
    Somalia / by Mary Virginia Fox.
        p. cm. -- (Enchantment of the world)
    Includes index.
    Summary: An overview of Africa's easternmost
country.
    ISBN 0-516-20019-4
    1. Somalia--Juvenile literature. [1. Somalia.] I. Title. II.
Series.
    DT401.5.F69 1996
    967.73--dc20   96-2025
                                               CIP
                                               AC

Photo credits ©: AP/Wide World Photos: 22 left, 67, 73
top left, 87, 94, 107 right; Archive Photos: 75 right, 91;
Audrey Gottlieb Photography: 19 right, 30, 38, 69 right, 73
top right; Robert Caputo/Aurora: cover, 58, 83, 88, 108;
The Bettmann Archive: 57 inset; The Bridgeman Art
Library: 12 (Giraudon), 44 (painting by Thomas Seddon);
Gamma-Liaison: 25 top right (Daniel J. Cox), 76 right (Eric
Girard), 33 (Wendy Stone), 32 (Edwards/Spooner); Greg
Marinovich: 6, 20 right, 28, 34, 36, 37, 39, 60 right, 64 top,
68 right, 68 left, 73 bottom right, 73 middle left, 77 left, 79,
80, 81, 90; Jay Mallin: 15, 69 top left; Anthony Ray/JB
Pictures: 92, 107 left; Jason Lauré / Lauré Communi-
cations: 4, 9 right, 11, 13, 40, 47, 50, 54, 56, 70, 73 middle
right, 74, 78, 86 right, 97, 100, 103, 105, 110; National
Museum of African Art: 52; North Wind Picture Archives:
43, 45, 46, 48, 82; Panos Pictures: 5, 9 left, 72, 85 right, 89
(all photos Betty Press), 69 bottom left, 109 (both photos
Crispin Hughes), 10, 14, 18, 19 left, 21, 35, 66 left, 102 (all
photos Hamish Wilson), 7, 8, 20 left, 27, 66 right, 76 left
(all photos Jeremy Hartley), 61 right, 61 left, 71 right (all
photos Kitty Warnock), 71 left (Liba Taylor);
Sovfoto/Eastfoto: 85 left, (Tass); United Nations: 29, 59, 75
left, 77 right; UPI/Bettmann: 57 top, 86 left, 95, 99;
UPI/Corbis-Bettmann: 106; Visuals Unlimited: 22 right, 25
bottom right (both photos Joe McDonald), 60 left (John D.
Cunningham), 63 (Ken Lucas), 25 bottom left, 25 top left
(both photos Kjell B. Sandved), 16 (Pat Armstrong), 25
middle right (Walt Anderson).

Cover picture: A displaced persons' camp in Somalia

Residents of the rural village of Burojabo must make a living from lifeless soil.

TABLE OF CONTENTS

A woman of the Shabeelle River area obtains water from the river.

Chapter 1

THE PEOPLE

The sharp-pointed northeast corner of Africa, called the Horn of Africa, is the land of a people known as Somalis. The territory stretches from the interior border of the Ethiopian highlands to the coast along the sharp northeast corner of the continent. The point divides the Gulf of Aden from the Indian Ocean. Somalia consists largely of eroded ravine-slashed plateaus, seared bushland, and rubble-strewn volcanic desert.

Somalis have never taken borders too seriously. When looking for good pasture, the people establish a home where there is grass and water. Following European colonial occupation, much of the land the Somalis occupied was turned over to them to govern in a step toward independence. They now had land within artificial lines drawn on a map. These lines are hard to define in the desert and harder still for the people to comprehend.

Actually, many Somalis live on lands that are part of the nations of

Much of Somalia is arid land strewn with volcanic rubble.

7

The Somali nomadic herders follow their animals wherever the search for water takes them, regardless of national boundaries.

Djibouti, Kenya, and Ethiopia. Somalis define their national identity through their traditional heritage no matter whether they live in Somalia or neighboring countries. The government of the Republic of Somalia hopes someday to incorporate all Somalis under one flag. This hope already has led to war and bloodshed.

ONE CULTURE, ONE PEOPLE

Other African nations have had the difficult task of trying to unify different tribal and language groups under one leader. Somalis, on the other hand, are as culturally unified as their neighbors are diverse. They speak a common language, share a powerful devotion to the Islamic religion, and organize their community life around similar social institutions.

Even in appearance they prove a common heritage. Somalis are related to the Oromo, Danakil, and Afar tribes of Ethiopia in the north. They were influenced through intermarriage with the Bantu in the river sections of the south. They are a tall and handsome

A clan elder (left) exhibits the bushy hair common to many Somali males. Two city girls (right) wear their hair in traditional braids.

race with aquiline features and elongated heads. Their skin color ranges from coppery brown to dusky black.

Unmarried males have long been accustomed to wearing their bushy hair in elaborate crowns framing their faces, but they cut it short when taking a wife. Women and girls are more apt to braid their hair neatly in narrow rows.

Western influence, especially along the coast where international trade has taken place for centuries, has brought a gradual change in customs, but 75 percent of the Somali people are pastoral nomads. They migrate endlessly around the Horn of Africa traveling with their herds in search of pasture and water. For these wanderers, life has changed little over the centuries.

The struggle for survival against overwhelming challenges has bred an intensely proud and individualistic people. Driven by the poverty of their resources, there is intense competition for access

A nomad family uses a camel to carry their house, while the family members walk behind the goat herd.

to water and pasture, which can frequently lead to fighting. But they can offer, as desert dwellers often do, generous hospitality to strangers. The very word *So-maal* means "Go and milk my beast," a generous greeting. Yet they show qualities of toughness and shrewdness. They are quick to take up arms if they feel an injustice has been committed against any of their own clan.

There is a fatalism to the Somali outlook on life. Drought often brings hardship from one year to another, but their faith in God, coming down to them from their prophet Muhammad in the seventh century A.D., gives them a secure feeling that a more powerful being controls their destiny.

Sir Richard Burton, one of the first white men to explore the Horn, described the Somalis in his book, *First Footsteps in Africa*,

The critical need in refugee camps, as well as throughout the Horn of Africa, is for fresh, drinkable water.

published in 1856. "They are full of curiosity and travel the world accepting almost any job without feeling a sense of inferiority, perhaps because they believe they are superior to everyone else."

EARLIEST HISTORY

Because there are few archeological records, the prehistory of the area is clouded. But it is believed that the Horn of Africa has been inhabited for at least 100,000 years. A number of theories exist about its settlements and early inhabitants.

One theory suggests that migrants from the Caucasus Mountains of Eurasia passed through the Middle East to Egypt. Some intermarried with Bantu-speaking people from the central African lake region. Some moved westward and others south

Carvings from the wall of the Mortuary Temple of Queen Hatshepsut in Egypt show the soldiers she sent on an expedition to the Land of Punt (Somalia).

along the Nile and Ethiopian plateaus.

A second theory suggests that immigrants from southern Arabia came directly to the Red Sea area, with some moving north into Egypt and others turning south to the Horn.

Still others believe that peoples from Mesopotamia and the Persian Gulf invaded Arabia, which was inhabited by black Africans at the time. The Bantu-speaking groups were then largely displaced by pastoral people—first the Oromo, then the Afar, and lastly the Somali.

Somalia was known in ancient times as the Land of Punt. The name is mentioned both in the Bible and on Egyptian hieroglyphics. Over thirty-five hundred years ago, the Egyptian Queen Hatshepsut sent expeditions to gather the fragrant and medicinal resins of frankincense and myrrh, tapped from wild trees that bristled through the sandy soil on barren hillsides of Punt.

Only the narrow Gulf of Aden separates Arabia from the Horn of Africa. It can be traversed by both primitive and modern sailing vessels.

Descriptions of the northern region and its inhabitants were written by an anonymous Greek sailor about A.D. 60 and in Ptolemy's *Geography.* A Chinese source dating from the ninth century also mentions the area. By the tenth century, Arabs and Persian merchants had established a number of ports on the coast, connecting east Africa with southwest Asia and the Indies in an extensive trading network.

Evidence from the last ten centuries leaves no doubt that the gradual spread of the Somali from the shores of the Gulf of Aden to the plains of northern Kenya was a gradual but constant migration. But the Somali did not take over an entirely empty land. Instead, they met the ethnically related Oromo peoples and a mixture of negroid or Bantu people. The Bantu lived mainly in the fertile land between the Shabeelle and Jubba Rivers.

Oral traditions, particularly within the Digil and Rahanwayn

Somali clans who entered this area between the rivers from the north, corroborate this part of their history. Their oral history refers to frequent bloodshed and the acquisition of slaves.

The second groups of people encountered by the Somalis were known as Ribi and Boni (or Wa-Ribi and Wa-Boni). They were hunters and fishermen. By about the tenth century, it seems that these two peoples were in contact with the Oromo people, who were already under pressure from the expanding Somali in the northeast corner of the Horn. Arab geographers in this early period often referred to the Oromo and Somali of the north as Berberi, to distinguish them in physical features and culture from the Zanj, who lived to the south.

As Arabs settled along the coasts, they introduced more sophisticated agriculture and a more centralized form of government. However, the most important result of Somali contact with the Arab world was the introduction of the Islamic faith.

Even before the Islamic period, Arabs and Persians across the Persian Gulf were developing a string of coastal settlements. Typical of these early Arab centers in northern Somalia are the ancient ports of Zeila and Berbera. The most important was the walled town of Zeila, sometimes called Seylac. After the sixth century, this town developed as a center for the coffee and ivory trade brought from the Abyssinian (Ethiopian) highlands and as a market for slaves brought from the Arab outpost of Harer in the interior. Other export items included hides and skins, ostrich feathers, and ghee, a kind of liquid butter. These items were frequently traded for cloth, dates, iron, weapons, and pottery.

Arabs established a similar series of ports to the south. Most important among them were Brava, Marka, and Mogadishu, today's capital. The traders usually arrived as comparative aristocrats, married local women, and eventually merged with the Somali culture.

Whichever theory of the Somali's origin is accepted, it is true that the Somali today represent a homogeneous people with strong feelings of unity. This unity will continue to play an important role in the story of the region.

Ghee, the liquid butter from herded animals, was among the early exports of the Somalis. Today, it is still a staple in the stores.

Chapter 2

THE LAND

With a population of about seven million people, Somalia cannot be regarded as a large nation. Yet the Somali form one of the largest ethnic groups in Africa.

Somalia is the cap of the geographic region called the Horn of Africa, which also includes Ethiopia and Djibouti. Its borders end at the edge of the Ethiopian highlands to the west, at the coast on the Gulf of Aden—often called the Eritrean coast—and Indian Ocean to the east—called the Benadir coast—and along the Tana River bordering Kenya to the south. The country covers 246,200 square miles (637,650 square kilometers), about the size of Texas, with a coastline of 1,839 miles (2,960 kilometers).

Geographically, Somalia is a land of limited contrast. In the north, paralleling the Gulf of Aden, is a plain that varies in width from about 35 miles (56 kilometers) in the west to as little as 1 or 2 miles (1.6 or 3.2 kilometers) in the east. Scrub-covered, semi-arid, and generally drab in appearance, this plain is known as the *Guban*, meaning "burned land." Most of the year it is seared with heat, and there is little rain to moisten the parched soil. When the rains do come, green vegetation appears briefly—just enough to

Opposite: A rare giraffe munches on the top leaves of a tree, while a dust devil forms in the dry land.

The foothills of the Golis Mountains provide more hospitable land than much of Somalia.

provide some short-lived grazing for nomadic livestock.

Away from the Gulf of Aden, the land gradually rises to a wall of cliffs that bisect the highlands. The Golis and Ogo mountains, with their steep escarpments, dominate the whole physical landscape of Somalia. They extend eastward from the northwestern border with Ethiopia to the tip of the Horn. Here they end in a steep drop at Cape Guardafui. The country's highest point, Surud Ad, which rises to over 7,900 feet (2,408 meters), is located near the town of Erigavo.

To the south, the mountains descend like steep stairs through a region known to the Somali as the Ogo. It is a region of shallow plateau valleys and usually dry riverbeds. It merges into an elevated plateau that is especially arid. There is not even one dry riverbed, a sign that for many a millennium there has not been enough rainfall to gouge even a trace in the sandy and rocky soil. This area in central Somalia is known as the Mudug Plain. In the

Eroded cliffs at the edge of the high plateau give eerie shapes to the steep escarpments (left). As dry as the Nugaal Valley (right) is, it is still home to livestock-herding nomads.

eastern section near the Indian Ocean, the Nugaal Valley gives signs that although rainfall is scarce, erratic storms once carved the landscape. It is the home of pastoral nomads.

The western part of the plateau is characterized by shallow valleys and seasonally dry watercourses. Just below the surface of the ground, there is a limited supply of water. Here, herders and farmers have dug wells that they return to during the dry season.

The western plateau slopes gently southward and merges into a broad rolling expanse that offers some of the best grazing land in the country. The natural depressions of the landscape fill with water during periods of rain, making temporary ponds for livestock and humans to use. This area has often been referred to as the Somali tableland, but, as one traveler described it, it is more like a table turned upside-down. Ravines have cut so deeply into the land that moving from one point to another is like climbing the legs of a table.

The Haud is a wild, waterless region that supports little life (left). The Shabeelle River (right), in southern Somalia, is a haven for parched people and cattle.

To the south of the city of Hargeysa, which was once the capital of the British Somaliland Protectorate, the plateau opens into the vast wilderness of thorn-bush and tall grasses known as the Haud. In the northern part of the country, the name *Haud* simply means "south." The region, which contains no water, extends into the Harer Province of Ethiopia.

Farther south, the plain tips gradually to the Indian Ocean. Here, it is intersected by valleys lined with welcome vegetation. Somalia's most important agricultural region is this area between the Shabeelle and Jubba rivers as they flow from the Ethiopian highlands. In addition, both the Shabeelle and Jubba rivers are lined in places with narrow borders of substantial forests.

The Shabeelle, or "Leopard," River extends for some 1,250 miles (2,012 kilometers), but it does not enter the sea. It flows eastward as far as Balad, 20 miles (32 kilometers) from the Indian

The Jubba River, which keeps the land around it green most of the year, is the only river in Somalia that is navigable from the sea.

Ocean coast, and then veers southward 170 miles (274 kilometers) more before it finally disappears in a series of marshes and sand flats close to Jelib on the Jubba River. Only during unusually heavy rainfall does the Shabeelle River ever join the Jubba and finally reach the sea.

The Jubba River, in contrast, flows more directly from the Ethiopian highlands to the sea, which it enters as a wide river near the port of Kismaayo. It is navigable by shallow-draft vessels from its mouth as far as the rapids.

CLIMATE

Climate affects every phase of Somali life. Over most of the land there are four seasons: two that bring some rain and two that are totally dry. The difference in weather is caused by the

Fortunately, flash floods such as this one in Mogadishu (left) are rare. Unfortunately, the more common dry weather (right) results in dust storms that can almost conceal the wildlife.

northeast and southwest monsoon winds and the transitional lulls between them that result in alternating wet and dry periods.

During the longest periods of monsoon air flow, winds blow parallel to the coast bringing little rainfall. In the first period, starting in late December or early January, hot, dry, and dusty winds are prevalent. This season, known locally as the *jilal,* lasts until about March. It is the harshest time of the year for nomads.

Beginning in March or April and extending into May, a transitional period known as *gu,* during which the winds change direction, brings the country's heaviest rains. Even in the best of years, the precipitation is meager. The third season, *hagaa,* begins in June. By July, pastures and vegetation begin to dry up and dust storms are frequent. This season continues through August and is the hottest period of the year in the north along the Gulf of Aden. Along the southwest coast, however, cooling breezes from the Indian Ocean help break the heat.

The second wet season, called *dayr,* is shorter, but its intermittent rains account for 30 percent of the annual rainfall. Most of the country receives under 20 inches (50 centimeters) of rain annually.

The mean daily maximum temperatures throughout the country range from 86° to 104° F. (30° to 40° C). The mean daily minimum temperatures usually vary from 68° to more than 86° F. (20° to more than 30° C).

FORESTRY

The country's forests, which are broadly defined as areas of vegetation dominated by trees of any size, cover as little as 13.7 percent of the land area. Little timber is produced. Most of the cut trees are used as firewood. However, frankincense and myrrh—both gum resins used in making perfume—are obtained from forests in the northeast. These important exports help to bring in foreign currency.

Plans have been set up to protect and restore Somali forests, but only limited progress has been made. Trial plantings of teak, gmelina (an Australian hardwood), mahogany, and eucalyptus were started. In the coastal area of southern Somalia, where sanddune drifting caused by overgrazing has been a problem, narrow bands of trees have taken root.

WILDLIFE

Like many other African countries, humans and their livestock are encroaching on the grazing and hunting space of wild animals. Somalia still has a large variety of big game and smaller wild animals, but their numbers have been greatly reduced since humans started taking count. Domesticated animals have driven game from the country's scarce watering spots, and the cutting of trees has destroyed the natural cover used by other animals.

The greatest pressure on large game animals has been the growth of the human population. Humans try to live on land that has always offered only limited resources for survival. When it comes to competition between humans and animals, the humans usually win.

Surveys done as early as 1964 and 1968 already showed the decrease of large animals in the north. Various kinds of antelope, as well as elephant, rhinoceros, and giraffe, were completely gone. Other formerly abundant species, including several gazelles, dik-dik (a small antelope), kudu (a large antelope with great spiral horns), lion, and wild donkey were greatly reduced.

In early 1969, game laws were strengthened, and a number of reserves were set aside to protect native species. There are still some big plant-eating animals, such as elephant, giraffe, black rhinoceros, buffalo, and zebra, in southwestern Somalia. Hippopotamuses inhabit the waters of the Jubba and Shabeelle rivers. In waters along the coast, a few dugong, which are similar to Florida's manatee, still survive, but they are an endangered species. Somalia's wild donkey, or ass, is also on the verge of disappearing. Only the antelopes and gazelles seem able to compete in large numbers for forage.

Large cats include the leopard, cheetah, lion, serval, and lynx. There are also fox, jackal, hyena, and wild dogs. Common small animals include mongoose, badger, and squirrel.

The natural balance of animals living in the area has been

Animals of Somalia, in addition to the less common zebras and giraffes, include: (clockwise from top right): wallowing hippopotamuses in the few rivers, warthogs, the dreaded black mamba, the vulturine guinea fowl, and the little antelope called the dik-dik.

severely upset with the hunting of the leopard and cheetah for their much-prized skins. This hunting has led to a substantial increase in the population of monkeys and warthogs that would have naturally been dinner for the larger animals. The monkeys and warthogs have, in turn, caused a great deal of damage to human agriculture.

Humans have to be constantly on the alert for snakes, including the dangerous puff adder, spitting cobra, and mamba. Pythons are also common in the southwest part of the country. Crocodiles are found in the water of the Jubba and Shabeelle rivers, and monitor lizards and large sea turtles are seen closer to coastal waters.

Houseflies, ants, and cockroaches thrive during the rainy season, and mosquitoes carry deadly malaria. Scorpions, ticks, sand flies, and, at certain times of the year, locusts, are also abundant.

A surprising number of birds, as many as 450 different species and subspecies, make their home in Somalia at least part of every year. About half migrate each year from eastern Europe and eastern Mediterranean countries and Asia Minor to make this their winter quarters. Where there is water, there are ducks, geese, pelicans, herons, flamingos, cormorants, and ospreys. Eagles, vultures, owls, hawks, and ravens are birds of prey. Game birds that are much sought after for food include guinea fowl, grouse, bustard, dove, and partridge. Even the ostrich is found on the open plain.

FISHING

In spite of their extensive coastline, Somalis traditionally dislike fish and disdain people who eat fish. Only those living

Available water has been taken over for livestock, preventing the larger wild mammals from finding what they need to survive.

along the rivers and southern coastal areas make seafood part of their diet. In the 1970s, the government unsuccessfully tried to develop a market for ocean produce.

The Banjuni, who live in the area, have developed a special method of catching turtles. A trained sucker fish attached to a line clamps onto the turtle's shell. The fisherman reels in both turtle and fish, and after removing the turtle, repeats the process. The shells of both turtles and tortoises are sold in the markets, but the

A small commercial fishing industry functions on the Indian Ocean coast even though Somalis in general do not eat much fish.

meat of the small reptiles is rarely eaten.

A Norwegian survey estimates that there is an ample supply of anchovies, sardines, herring, tuna, and mackerel in the nearby waters. Bottom-dwelling fish include flounder, groupers, porgies, and snappers. Sharks and rays are abundant.

Commercial fishing is affected by the rocky, uneven character of the sea bottom of the relatively narrow continental shelf around Somalia. As a result, trawling and netting are possible only in select areas. Monsoon winds during a good part of the year cause heavy seas that make fishing by small craft unsafe.

In spite of these difficulties, the government has sponsored several projects to encourage the Somali fishing industry. A fishing cooperative was set up in 1971. Fish not used locally were salted

and sold to the government monop-
oly cooperative, Somalfish. New
mechanized boats were purchased,
but with few trained mechanics and
a shortage of parts, the fishing fleet
quickly shrank.

Four new fishery settlements
were established along the coast in
the mid-1970s. Fifteen thousand
nomads who were starving because
of the drought of 1974-1975 were
resettled there to give them a new
form of livelihood. The people, taken
away from the territory they felt
belonged to their clan ancestors, had
difficulty adjusting.

In 1977 ten Soviet trawlers
equipped to freeze catches reported
taking 9,670 tons (8,772 metric tons)
of fish. But as soon as there was a
political break between Somalia
and the Soviet Union, the ships
withdrew. In 1981 Somalia licensed
several Italian and Iraqi trawlers to
fish the waters. So far, the results
have been disappointing, and with
today's internal conflicts, there have
been no government funds to
subsidize the industry.

*A proud Somali fisherman shows off
his catch.*

Although this woman is wearing a hat that says "Somalia," she is likely to owe her main allegiance to her clan-family.

Chapter 3

KINSHIP GROUPS

Somali social and political organization has long been based on kinship groups, including six main clan-families, which are further subdivided into smaller clans. The clans, in turn, are subdivided into subclans, or primary lineage groups.

SAMAAL AND SAAB

All Somali are said to trace their origin to two brothers, Samaal and Saab. They are thought to have been members of the Prophet Muhammad's tribe, the Quraysh of Arabia. It is hard to prove these claims, but Somalis assert them with a distinct pride.

Of the six clan-families, four—the Dir, the Darod, the Isaq, and the Hawiye—make up approximately 75 percent of the population. They trace their descent from Samaal. Most still live the nomadic life.

The Digil and the Rahanweyn, on the other hand, trace their ancestry through Saab. They rely on a mixed economy of cattle-raising and farming. They make up about 20 percent of Somalis.

Despite their common background, the Samaal and the Saab developed different patterns of social and political life. Part of this difference was caused by the area of the country where they made their homes. The Samaal roamed the area west of the Jubba River where pasture would support only camels, sheep, and goats. The

Cattle thrive best when they do not have to be herded to water sources. The two Saab clan-families settled on land near the two rivers to raise cattle and crops.

Saab lived in the area between the Shabeelle and Jubba rivers, where they raised cattle. Because cattle do not give much milk during the hot dry season, the Saab turned to cultivating the land, exchanging what crops they grew with their neighbors. This changed the social order of their lives.

The Samaal regard each of their group as equals. The Saab, on the other hand, developed a complicated ranking system. The Samaal who wander take pride in the history of their ancestors. The greater the number of generations between a person and the ancestor, the greater the prestige. Some ancient clans, however, have dwindled in numbers and have had to attach themselves to segments of other clan-families. Also, small groups that were detached in distance from the main body of their clan often arrange a protective alliance, called a *fashanbur,* meaning "pile of shields," because the agreement guarantees a certain amount of protection if there is serious trouble.

The Samaal nomads practice what has been described as "pastoral democracy," without permanent chiefs or formal courts.

The larger group of clan-families belong to the Samaal, who have continued to act as nomadic herders of camels, goats, and sheep.

Whatever order is established is carried out in the *shir,* an assembly composed of all the adult males in a certain lineage group. Each of the males might speak and take part in the deliberation, but age and seniority of lineage take precedence.

The Samaal keep a careful count of their ancestors and rarely adopt strangers. Samaal consider their status as herders and warriors to be nobler than any other, with the exception of those devoting themselves to religion. The Saab who cultivated the soil had the distinction of ownership of land, yet over the years they have been looked down upon by the Samaal.

Pastureland is thought of as God's gift to all, but wells are considered to belong to the man who is responsible for having them dug and to his ancestors.

THE POLITICS OF OWNERSHIP

Clans are still the largest political units within Somalia. Most have heads known as *soldaan,* or "sultans," who serve a largely

Elders of a clan sit in judgment on many aspects of clan life. All adult males are expected to participate.

ceremonial function. The title, from the Arabs, means the same as the Somali term *bokor,* meaning "to bind people together."

The number of clans within a clan-family varies. Clans are associated with a given territory, defined by the usual path of migration, and not by specific boundaries. Often these circuits overlap so that there are conflicting claims. Some clans have joined in confederations to protect their interests.

The right of ownership is not always clear, because more than one clan migrates over a given territory, and intermarriage frequently clouds official titles. There is often harsh fighting over the possession of water sources, which are essential to the survival of their flocks and ultimately to the herdsmen and families.

Samaal are known for their aggressiveness. Continual battles would result if it were not for the *dia*-paying groups, which make peaceful settling of disputes possible. Dia-paying groups are formed by agreements, or contracts, among close kinsmen, usually within the same subclan, for the purpose of paying or receiving

This sheik is the head, or the sultan, of a clan.

compensation, or dia, in case of homicide resulting from competition between their group and others. Dia may be one hundred camels for a man and fifty for a woman. The part of the compensation given to the immediate kin of a murdered man or paid by the immediate kin of the man responsible is known as *jiffo.*

"Immediate kin" refers to those who claim common ancestry three or four generations back. The immediate kin may contract within the dia-paying group to carry the financial burden of the jiffo, often a third of the dia payment, as a kind of insurance. Loyalty is then to the group guaranteeing protection.

Both dia-paying groups and jiffo-paying groups are important units of social and economic life. They function as mutual-aid groups in time of emergency. The groups are ruled by the elders in council, who settle disputes sometimes quite forcibly. If a man refuses to pay his share of camels for a fine, he may be tied to a tree while his livestock is killed one by one in front of him.

MARRIAGE

Marriage is not only a religious ceremony, it is a contract of economic and political importance. The marriage is seen as a political bond between lineages or dia-paying groups. To validate the marriage, a standard series of payments is negotiated by the

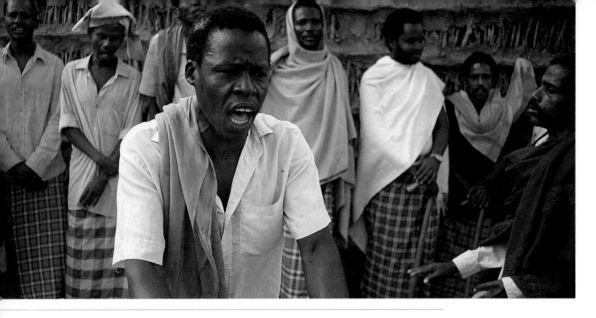

Men sing to celebrate a marriage between different clan groups.

elders representing the bride and groom. Marriage within a lineage group is forbidden. If a couple is separated by six or more generations within the lineage, however, marriage is usually accepted. However, it may be frowned on because it does not create any advantageous new relationship between groups.

A wife never legally becomes a member of her husband's lineage. It is her father's, and not her husband's, dia-paying and jiffo-paying groups that pay for or receive fines on her behalf. Yet her children belong to her husband's lineage.

Samaal look down on Saab for their readiness to bring foreign elements into their lineage groups. Saab clans are roughly the same size as Samaal clans but are really confederations of lineages, probably made up of representatives of all Somali clan-families. The clans tend to have only a small core of the original group that bore the name and a larger proportion of intermarried or adopted members. Because of their diversity, Saab typically marry within their group, following the Arab practice of preferential marriage of

These Saab people live in the region between the Shabeelle and Jubba rivers, where their ancestors settled.

a man with his father's brother's daughter, so that inheritance stays within the family rather than spreading across family ties.

SAAB SOCIAL LEVELS

Another important difference between Samaal and Saab is that Saab clans live within clearly marked territorial areas. Clan affairs are handled by leading elders called *gobwein,* who have assistants called *gobyar.* The lineage of the clan members denotes their economic status. The headmen decide who owns land and water rights.

In contrast to the Samaal, there are decidedly different social levels in Saab society. At the top of the rank are the descendants of the original clan, the treatymakers. They are called *urad* (first-born) or *mindihay* (knife-bearer). Traditionally, they officiate at all joint clan activities, such as the rainmaking ceremony called *roobdoon,* and they ritually slaughter animals for sacrifice, in rituals dating

Such tasks as basket-weaving may be the work of specific clans.

back before Islam was embraced.

Lower on the social scale are "former clients," a term used for trading partners. They were often small, weak, and more recent arrivals in the territory. At first they were not permitted to own land, dig wells, or build permanent housing. Only after they had proved to be an asset to the group were they allowed to participate in councils and become members of the dia-paying groups.

In Saab society, certain occupations are assigned to certain families. There are also occupational groups who do not belong to clans. Instead, they serve their Samaal or Saab "patrons." However, they keep accurate records of their own family trees and have their own customs. Some have no fixed homesites, but wander where their services are needed. For example, the Yibir medicine men make protective charms for newborns, warriors, and newly married couples. The Tumal are blacksmiths, the Dardown are weavers, and the Madarrala and the Gaggab are tanners and shoemakers.

Those who are hunters, leather dressers, smiths, and medicine men are regarded as being low in caste. The largest low-caste group is the Midgaan, who act as barbers and circumcisers. They also act as hunters, but the government has restricted this activity since 1970.

38

OTHER KINSHIP GROUPS

Along the coast of the Indian Ocean and in the valleys of the Jubba and Shabeelle rivers, there are small groups of a distinctly different people, called the Habasho. Today they speak the Somali language, but many believe that these people are descendants of liberated slaves who successfully defended themselves against the Somali. The nomads regard the Habasho with respect because they have been able to take care of themselves under harsh conditions where insects have brought disease. Somali nomads maintain treaties with these people so that they can pass through the land on their way to water their flocks.

Neither the Habasho nor Somali ever intermarry, nor do they eat together. But they often enter into "client-patron" relationships, with the river people often acting as cultivators for the herdsmen. Many Habasho have converted to Islam but retain old customs, such as using animal masks in their rituals.

Along the coast live the Banjuni and Amerani. These groups have a distinct culture of their own and speak an entirely different language. They live lives related to the sea, perhaps as fishermen, sailors, or merchants.

This Habasho man blowing on a shell lives along the coast.

Even the simplest of sea-going craft, such as this Indian Ocean dhow, could carry foreigners across the Red Sea or the Gulf of Aden from the Middle East. Europeans arrived in larger ships and had an even greater impact on the recent history of the Horn of Africa.

Chapter 4

FOREIGNERS ARRIVE

Somalia's location on the Horn of Africa has made it vulnerable to attacks by other countries in the region, and even by powers with navies that traveled through the Red Sea. The earliest Somali conflicts, however, were local battles, neighbors against neighbors. Then, by the thirteenth century, a large number of Somalis were drawn into full-scale wars.

Somalis have rarely been able to claim complete isolation and independence. Even before the countries of Europe expanded their appetites to place large segments of the world's population under their rule, Somalis had contact with their Arabian, Ethiopian, and Egyptian neighbors. But none of them played a formal role in controlling Somalia until powerful Great Britain became so strong in the region that Ethiopia and Egypt had to prove their domination with force.

THE ARABS IN SOMALIA

During the thirteenth century, the Islamic state of Ifat, which included Adal and the port of Zeila, was ruled by the Walashma, an Arab dynasty. As they prospered and became stronger, they sought to enlarge their kingdom, especially in the direction of Ethiopia, then called Abyssinia. The Sultan of Ifat, Haq ad-Din, called up an army to wage a religious war against the Abyssinian

41

A Portuguese map created in 1508 shows clearly the Horn of Africa and even indicates the location of Mogadishu.

"infidels." During their first success, churches were destroyed and Christians were forced to renounce their religion at the point of a sword. However, in 1415 the ruler of Ifat, Sa'd ad-Din, was killed and his army destroyed. While the Abyssinians sang songs to celebrate their victory, the Muslims eulogized Sa'd ad-Din as a martyr.

Sa'd ad-Din's sons fled to Arabia where they found refuge with the king of Yemen. But after a few years, they returned to occupy some of their former territory. The Walashma dynasty then assumed the title of "Kings of Adal" and moved their capital to Dakkar, farther from the threat of Abyssinian attack. After almost a hundred years of peace, an Arab leader, Ahmad Ibrahim al-Ghazi—called Ahmad Gran—led his forces in ferocious attacks against his Christian neighbors. He was equipped with cannon furnished by mysterious allies and imported through the port of Zeila.

At that time, the Majerteyn Darod clan controlled much of the northeast coast of Somalia. The Darod clan played an important role in these battles. The Darods further strengthened their ties with the Arab leaders by the marriage between a sister of the Arab *imam*, or spiritual leader, and one of the Darod leaders.

The imam used his power, both spiritual and military, to band

Portuguese explorer Vasco da Gama was the first European to reach Somalia by some route other than through Arabia. His son, Pedro, later helped the Abyssinians fight against Muslim invaders from Somalia.

the northern Somalis together. Most of the time, they had been too occupied with hostilities among family groups to put aside their grievances and unite for a single cause. But the strength of Muslim power was again challenged. The Abyssinians turned for help to the Portuguese, who were at the height of their naval and trading power in the Red Sea. The Muslims sought support from the Turks.

In 1542 the imam was killed, and Muslim power was suppressed. In the meantime, Oromo people swept through Abyssinia, killing Muslim and Christian alike. This left Somali clans to defend themselves. Again, they rarely joined to fight battles that did not ultimately affect their own daily lives. Their main concern was simple survival.

By the eighteenth century, groups of the Dir clan, who had been pushed from their homes in the east and center of Somalia, had settled as far south as the Jubba River. Other clans were vying for the land, and battles were frequent. The Darod clan sought alliances with the Oromo, and for a while there was peace.

In 1865, a German traveler, Klaus von der Decken, who attempted to sail up the Jubba River in a shallow-draft steamship,

British adventurer Sir Richard Burton became the first known white man to reach parts of Somalia. He later became most famous for his translation into English of The Arabian Nights.

recorded that the Oromo had been stricken with a severe epidemic of smallpox. Almost immediately, the Darod clan took advantage of the weakness of their enemies to take control of the area stretching down into what is now northern Kenya. Many who remained were made slaves, or at least servants, of the Somali overlords. It was only through the force of European colonial powers that the migration of the Somalis was stopped.

GROWING EUROPEAN INFLUENCE

Even after the decline of the state of Adal, Zeila remained an important link in the ancient caravan routes from the interior, particularly from the Abyssinian highlands through Harer. During the following century, Zeila, and to some extent Berbera, fell under the authority of the Arabs, and were nominally incorporated into the Ottoman Empire.

The British were beginning to look at Somalia from across the Gulf of Aden. By the time explorer Sir Richard Burton visited the

Sir Richard Burton's camp in the desert was attacked by Somali fighters determined to destroy a treaty that allowed the British to trade in the area.

Somali coast in 1854, Zeila's governor was a Somali of the Habar Yunis clan. He had earned the friendship of the British government by protecting the lives of the crew of the *Mary Ann,* a British brig attacked and plundered by local Somalis at Berbera.

Because of the *Mary Ann* incident, a commercial treaty was signed between the British East Africa Company and the Habar Awal clan. However, the treaty did not guarantee peace. On April 19, 1855, several hundred Somali spearmen launched a ferocious attack upon Burton's camp. One of Burton's men was killed, and Burton and another man were wounded. The British authorities stationed at Aden, across the Gulf of Aden, promptly blockaded the coast until the attackers surrendered. It was announced that the guilty one who had led the attack had been killed by his own people. In addition, fifteen thousand dollars in cash was paid to the British government. Now the link between Aden and the northern coast of Somalia was strengthened, and the base was laid for future British activity.

Troops of the Sultan of Zanzibar, who controlled the Mogadishu area in the 1800s, performed a war dance, prior to attack.

Meanwhile, the southern Somali coast had also come under European influence. Mogadishu had begun in the tenth century as a loose federation of Arab and Persian families. By the thirteenth century, it was ruled by the Somali sultan of the Fakhr ad-Din dynasty. Three centuries later, these rulers were supplanted by the Muzaffar sultans. The town was attacked by Portuguese sailors but never captured. The real conquerors of the ancient port were the newly arrived settlers of the Hawiye clan.

At this time, the Arab influence from the country of Oman was very strong, dominating all trade in the Indian Ocean. By the close of the seventeenth century, Mogadishu and the other East African ports had come under the protection of Oman. Mogadishu then lost its influence and was reduced to a town of 5,000 under the control of Zanzibar, governed by two men, one a Somali and the other an Arab who spoke some English.

To the north, the Benadir ports of Marka, Brava, and Kismaayo, which faced the Indian Ocean while having connections with Oman, remained politically independent. Zeila and Berbera were

The influence of the sultanate, or Ottoman Empire, is still clearly seen in the buildings on Lamu Island, which lies on the border of Kenya with Somalia.

still formally part of the Turkish Ottoman Empire, though both were heavily involved with trade with the British at Aden.

Thus, by the middle of the nineteenth century, the Somali coast was no longer isolated. Outside influences were at work. With the European scramble for African territories, Somalia's independence —always under threat—was about to be challenged by even more powerful forces.

COLONIAL RULE

The British were concerned about guaranteeing meat supplies from Somalia for their naval base across the Gulf of Aden. Aden was a splendid port, but it had no resources of its own. The other powers who were interested in the area had broader imperial ambitions.

In 1859 France bought the port of Obock from the Danakil clan of Somalia. It was not until 1881, eleven years after the opening of the Suez Canal, that France took advantage of her possession by

European influence in the Gulf of Aden began in the early 1500s when ships such as this were used by the Portuguese to capture Aden. From there it was a short step across the gulf to Somalia.

setting up the Franco-Ethiopian Trading Company. Also, in 1869, the port of Assab on the Red Sea coast was purchased by an Italian shipping company, which proposed to run services through the Suez Canal and the Red Sea to India.

Egypt, not to be outdone, revived her claim to the Somali coast. Muhammad Jamal Bey was sent to raise the Egyptian flag over Bulhar and Berbera. This upset the British, who did not wish to see any other power established on the opposite shore of the Gulf of Aden from their own naval base. However, the British Parliament was not ready to resort to war to clear the area. So in time, Britain came to regard the Egyptian occupation of the land opposite Aden as better than if another European power had obtained there. A treaty was drawn up in 1877 whereby the British recognized Egyptian jurisdiction as far south as Ras Hafun.

The Egyptians had little difficulty establishing their authority over the ports of Zeila, Bulhar, and Berbera. They greatly improved the port facilities of both Zeila and Berbera. Piers and lighthouses were erected, and at Berbera the ancient Dunbar aqueduct was rebuilt to supply fresh water to the town.

Egyptian influence over the nomads was more limited. While

the Somalis still considered themselves to be independent, there was no consolidated effort to drive out the foreigners. At this time, the Somalis had no firearms. They had to depend solely on spears and daggers for fighting. Most importantly, they were not united. In fact, they were often divided by bitter inter-clan feuds.

During the 1870s, a modest degree of order was maintained on the Somali coast by Egyptian forces. However, Africans from the Sudan were pressing Egyptians at other borders. When it became clear that the Egyptians would have to pull out of Somalia, the British prepared to fill the void by negotiating a treaty with the Somalis.

Somali clans were used to such contractual alliances between clans. They readily agreed. No land was ceded, although Somalis promised not to sell or give up any of their territory except to the British government, if at some time in the future land titles were to change hands. The British promised the protection of Her Majesty the Queen Empress in case any of Somalia's neighbors tried to lay claim to Somali land. This new British Somaliland Protectorate included northern Somalia along the Gulf of Aden.

By 1884, the Egyptians had pulled out from the interior, leaving three British vice-consuls to guarantee order. They were to be aided by forty members of the Aden police and one hundred Somali coast police, who were quickly recruited and armed as caravan guards to protect the trade routes.

To the north, the French had negotiated a protectorate agreement with the part of the Issa clan that dominated Djibouti. This area was also claimed by the British. After many threats, the two powers finally decided on a compromise. Borders were redrawn on a map, but British authorities refused to allow French

The port of Djibouti was established by the French in 1888 in what was then French Somaliland. For some years the country was called Afars and Issas for the people inhabiting it. The Issas are a Somali clan-family. Today French Somaliland is the small, very poor country of Djibouti, located west of Somalia on the northern coast of the Horn of Africa.

transports to refuel with coal at Aden. It was up to France to establish her own base.

At the same time, Italy became interested in Somalia as a trading center. The Italians eased themselves into the city of Mogadishu with little resistance. Britain agreed to share power along the access to the Red Sea with relatively weak Italy in preference to its French rival. With British blessings, the Italians opened a second East Africa territory on the Indian Ocean along the Benadir coast between the Jubba River and the British Somaliland Protectorate.

While France was in the process of negotiating a bid for the Eritrean port of Massawa after the withdrawal of the Egyptian forces, Britain encouraged Italy to slip in and make the necessary arrangements with the Turks to take over the port. In 1889, Italy also became involved in acquiring Somali trading interests. This was not what the British had anticipated.

Without consulting Ethiopia, Britain and Italy agreed to treaties in 1891 and 1894 that defined the boundaries between their respective zones of influence. The inland boundaries placed the Ogaden region in the Italian sphere and the Haud region in the British sphere. In 1896, when the Italian forces invaded the Ethiopian highlands from Eritrea along the Red Sea coast, they were soundly defeated in the Battle of Adowa. Italy settled for Eritrea and its holdings in Somalia. Ethiopia already claimed control over much territory in which Somali nomads traditionally roamed, and it had obtained territorial concessions from the Italians in Eritrea and the French in Djibouti. Britain agreed to relinquish some of its claims to keep peace and to gain Ethiopia's good will. It was in no position to use force.

Somalia's present-day border with Kenya was a result of secret negotiations that brought Italy into World War I on the side of the Allies. A treaty drawn up in 1920 and ratified in 1924 gave Italy the area west of the Jubba River up to the forty-first parallel. The new boundary left a large area of land within the country of Kenya populated by Somali people.

THE "MAD MULLAH"

Before the start of the twentieth century, there was a major effort to rid Somalia of all outsiders. In 1899 the shaky peace among the colonial powers was shattered by a revolt led by Muhammad ibn Abdullah Hasan, the imam of the puritanical Salihiyyah sect. This mullah, or Islamic teacher, planned to get rid

An artist for the Illustrated London News *in 1901 dramatized the Mad Mullah's uprising by fantasizing how Somali trackers might search out the enemy.*

of all foreign influences that violated Islamic rules of behavior. He disapproved of the use of liquor, and he planned to banish a French-run Roman Catholic orphanage that had taken in Somali children. Muhammad Abdullah was a forceful orator and poet, much valued skills in Somali society. His followers were called *darwish* (dervish) to indicate their lack of clan affiliation.

The Somalis from the coastal towns were hard to impress. They had prospered from the improved opportunities of trade under colonial rule. But the imam won his converts from the nomads of the interior, especially from his own Dolbahants and Ogaden clans, both of which belonged to the Darod clan-family.

The revolt of the imam's followers was touched off by the

arrest of one follower accused of stealing a rifle. The colonial powers had sought to ban weapons from the Somalis. The tribesmen claimed they were deprived of a means of defending themselves against harassment by soldiers in the Ethiopian-controlled areas.

To secure weapons, the imam's followers began to attack caravans and engage in camel raids. The British, supported by Ethiopian forces, led four expeditions against the mullah but were unable to defeat him.

In 1910 the British government, unwilling to invest more manpower and supplies in the fight, withdrew to the coastal areas, abandoning the interior to the dervishes. The Somalis, whom the British had promised to protect, were issued rifles and left to defend themselves. Over the next few years, there was a bitter civil war, and the dervishes terrorized the whole region. It has been estimated that one-third of the men of British Somaliland were killed during this period.

During World War I, Muhammad Abdullah received German and Turkish support, including assistance in building military fortifications. The largest of these is at Taleh, towering 60 feet (18.3 meters) high with walls 14 feet (4.3 meters) thick. In 1920 the British air force bombed the dervish strongholds, but Muhammad escaped into Ethiopia, where he died that same year.

Today, Muhammad Abdullah is regarded by many as a national hero. Some say that he established a true Islamic state to reclaim his land from Christian invaders—British, French, Italian, and Ethiopian. Yet many of his own Somalis turned against him, tired of the chaos, death, and destruction he had caused. The British called Muhammad "the Mad Mullah," which described not only his political fervor but also his religious fanaticism.

The rocky terrain of Somalia often serves as a convenient, secret route for smugglers to carry drugs into neighboring Ethiopia.

Chapter 5

EUROPE TAKES OVER

After suppressing Muhammad Abdullah's revolt, Britain determined to extend its control to the borders of Ethiopia for security reasons. For the French as well as the British, the importance of gaining a foothold on the Horn of Africa stemmed from its location. It guards the shortest sea route from the Indian Ocean to Europe.

Italy expanded its territory during the same time but for very different reasons. The Italian government had plans for resettling farmers from Italy's poorer regions, and it also hoped that it could make profits by trading with Somalia and neighboring countries.

The first attempts at mechanized commercial agriculture occurred in the Shabeelle River valley. Bananas, sugarcane, and cotton were introduced as cash crops. However, the Somalis preferred to work on their own land instead of for wages, and the Italians had not brought in enough people to handle the projects proposed by their government.

Profitable trade was affected by the completion of the railroad connecting the French port of Djibouti with Addis Ababa in Ethiopia in 1917. The older trade routes were abandoned, and commerce flowed through other hands. Still, there was substantial economic development at this time.

When Benito Mussolini's Fascist regime came to power in Italy in 1922, there was a surge of construction. In Somalia, 3,728 miles

Trade with the outside world received a major boost from the Djibouti-to-Addis Ababa railroad.

(6,000 kilometers) of gravel roads were built, and a narrow-gauge railroad was built to connect the plantations in the south to Mogadishu. A certain amount of authority was given to Somalis. Somali judges were appointed to administer Islamic law, and a small number held minor clerical positions with the government. However, little was done to improve the average Somali's education level or health standards.

Economic development in British Somaliland was very slow during the period between the two world wars. The colonial administration was required to finance its operation from the country's own resources. Most revenue was spent on digging wells and building veterinary services. The British tried to expand a school system, but the plan received little support from the people. The conservative religious Somali sentiment considered British-sponsored education a threat to Islam.

WARTIME SOMALIA

Even before 1930, Italians had moved into the Somali-populated Ogaden area of Ethiopia. Although the boundaries had been

Benito Mussolini (right) took control of Italy and her colonies in 1922. In 1926, Italian troops took possession of Italian Somaliland after quieting a local uprising (above).

confirmed in a treaty of 1908, there were no permanent markers set up on the rocky soil. In 1934, Italian army troops provoked an armed confrontation with Ethiopian troops at Wal Wal, the site of wells used regularly by Somalis, although clearly inside Ethiopia.

The Italian dictator, Mussolini, used the incident as an excuse to invade farther into Ethiopia. Without a formal declaration of war, his troops captured the capital of Addis Ababa. The Ogaden was now added to an enlarged province of Somalia, which, together with Eritrea, made up Italian East Africa.

In early February of 1941, the British attacked the Italian forces in Somalia and took Mogadishu. British units based across the Gulf in Aden landed at Berbera. After Addis Ababa was taken in April, the last of the Italian forces in East Africa were compelled to surrender.

Ethnic Somalis demonstrate in the Ogaden region of Ethiopia. This part of the Horn of Africa has changed hands several times.

After World War II, a temporary British military authority was set up as a protectorate in both Somalia and the eastern part of Ethiopia. Thus, nearly all Somali people, except a small number in French Somaliland, were under British control. Yet Britain had its hands full on other fronts. Its main goal in Somalia was to provide law and order in the area. The Somaliland Camel Corps was reorganized to take control, and in the south, five battalions were under the command of British officers to police the area.

The tribal rural constabulary, called the *gogle,* were given back their power. The old clan chiefs and leaders continued to receive government subsidies, but when vacancies occurred, they were not replaced. Instead, tribal assemblies were encouraged to work with the administration. Elections for assemblies were held, and District and Provincial Advisory Councils were created in 1946.

Somali nomads in the interior took advantage of the windfall

The Somali Legislative Assembly building in Mogadishu features a mural symbolizing the union of British Somaliland and the UN Trust Territory, which the Italians administered.

in weapons they were able to gather and caused serious problems for the peacekeeping force. Under British military control, schools were set up, though it was difficult to find a qualified teaching staff. Though education was still pitifully inadequate, the number of children, almost entirely boys, attending school had doubled since before the war. Sanitation was improved, and a local court system reorganized. Somalis who qualified as junior officials in the civil service and police force had their first official training as Western politicians.

The first modern Somali political organization, the Somali Youth Club (SYC) was founded in Mogadishu in 1943. The club had thirteen founding members representing the main Somali clan groups. Religious leaders as well as laymen were included. In the beginning, most of SYC's support came from the younger educated officials and from the Somalia Gendarmerie, which was

Lush fruit plantations in the Shabeelle-Jubba region were among the benefits of European involvement in Somaliland (left). Today, many of these abandoned plantations are harvested by a few local people who sell the crops at roadside stands (above).

the new police force. By 1947, it had changed its name to the Somali Youth League and had no less than 25,000 members. A four-point program was drawn up to unite all Somalis, to educate all Somalis, and to set up a system of laws that would protect the interest of all Somalis.

A TIME OF CHANGE

Once law and order had been restored, the most pressing problem was restoring a favorable economic base. Many of the plantations on the Shabeelle and Jubba had been abandoned. The Somali labor force had virtually disappeared, and looting had caused widespread damage.

Somalis and Arabs were encouraged to make use of the better

Hargeysa, the former capital of British Somaliland, is an old trading city in which many of the oldest parts (left) have been destroyed by war. The newer city (right) has a thriving meeting place in the center of town.

land. Loans for tractor fuel were granted. The production of sugar and grains was encouraged. New councils were set up to discuss such problems as water supply, food scarcities, and health needs. However, a plague of locusts in 1944-45 devastated the land. Camels and cattle died of starvation, their owners soon to follow.

During the period between the end of World War II and independence, there was a gradual social and economic change. Somalis who were well educated in the Islamic tradition tried to do away with the divisions along clan lines. One of the first acts of the SYL-dominated assembly in 1956 was to make it illegal for political parties to be named after clan-families. A conscious effort was made to bring members of ethnic minorities into the mainstream of political life.

A law was passed abolishing the status of "client." This was a term that literally meant "share cropping." Those who owned the land by right of inheritance would, in fact, hire others to work it for a share of the produce. The law tried to give this land to those working it. Naturally, this was against the former client-patron arrangements, and landowners simply refused to give up their rights. Little was done to uphold the new law.

Social change was more pronounced in the towns. Somali towns are of two sorts—those with a history dating back a thousand years and those that grew around newer administrative centers and trading markets. The older coastal towns were usually dominated by one or two clans with no direct kin-based relationships with the surrounding area. The newer towns often were connected to clans in neighboring areas, and occasionally disagreements would arise over land use.

In the past, those with certain occupational skills had been looked down upon. Many Tumal, for example, became mechanics and settled in towns. Now many of these skills were needed. They were no longer considered bondsmen, or indentured servants, to other clans. They were independent and often formed their own guilds to protect their interests.

Although the lives of city dwellers had changed dramatically as they came in contact with other cultures and countries, they still remained close to their country cousins. Nomad families frequently had one or more members living in the city earning money that helped pay for building up the family herds.

There was an international effort in the works to make Somalia independent, but the wheels of diplomacy were slow. In 1949, the United Nations General Assembly discussed the disposal of the colonies owned by Italy, which had been on the losing end of World War II. A compromise plan was drawn up which, surprisingly, entrusted most of Somalia for the next ten years to Italian administration. However, the Assembly laid down enough firm provisions to prevent another Fascist dictatorship.

The Ogaden and Haud areas of the interior were given back to Ethiopia. The plan to incorporate a Greater Somalia according to the areas now inhabited by these culturally united people lacked international support.

The British were granted a continuing responsibility in what had been, and would continue to be, the British Protectorate of Somaliland. There was further expansion of schools. Experiments with new crops and fertilizers were initiated, and a couple of small experimental date plantations were established. The conservative Somalis resisted change, but change would come.

As Somalia was preparing for great changes when World War II was ending, it was devastated by a locust plague that destroyed all crops in 1944-45. Camels and cattle died of starvation, and so, too, did their owners.

Above: In rural areas, thatched huts, or **muudul,** *of various shapes are built.*
Below: In coastal towns such as Brava, classical white-washed houses are built close to the water.

Chapter 6

A WAY OF LIFE

Before independence and the bitter battles between clans that followed, Somali lives rarely changed from one generation to the next. There were periods of famine and despair, but lifestyles were dictated by where one lived. Houses varied from the collapsible dwellings of the nomads to the solid Italian-style villas in the big cities. There was a small elite group who owed their luxuries to government jobs. Their homes were usually made of large square hand-made bricks covered with plaster, set in the middle of spacious yards surrounded by high stone walls.

Arab-style houses are built one or two stories high but always with a flat roof that is used as a second living room to catch any breeze that might have a cooling effect. Metal grills or iron bars protect windows on the first floor. Rarely is there screening or glass. Although Europeans and Asians, mostly from India and Pakistan, generally gathered in certain areas, Somalis lived in all sections, with lavish homes and the most modest dwellings side by side.

During periods of drought, hundred of families converged on the coastal cities to find work and food. They built the kind of housing they were used to. Nomads set up elongated portable dwellings, called *agal,* which could be easily taken apart and transported by camel. They used poles or bundles of weeds to build the frames of their dwellings. An average house would

Among nomadic people, it is the task of the women to assemble the family dwelling (left). When drought conditions (right) drive nomads from their normal traveling routines, they may head for the cities.

measure about 10 feet (3 meters) across and 6 or 8 feet (1.8 to 2.4 meters) high. Hides or woven mats of sisal or other fibers were used to cover the outside, floor, and entrance.

The most important item in a nomad house is the bed, made of woven palm-leaf ribs supported on four wooden stakes and covered with skins. Household items include little more than leather water bags, decorated wooden vessels and mats, stools, headrests, camel bells, spoons, combs, and boxes for storing things as they are loaded on the camels.

Among the farmers who settled in one location, metal roofs were a sign of prosperity. Their household items could be heavier

Even on the outskirts of a major city like Mogadishu, the search for water during a period of drought can be never-ending . . . and sometimes hopeless.

and more permanent than those of nomads. Rough wooden furniture, pottery and hollowed gourds, and woven bags are prized possessions.

People from settled rural areas usually built a one-room muudul, a circular framework of slender poles and vines that they plastered with a mixture of mud, ashes, and dung. A 9-foot (2.7-meter) center pole supported a dunce-cap thatched roof.

Once the newcomers to a town decided to stay, they frequently built an *arish,* a rectangular house made in the same way as the muudul. It might be as large as 20 by 40 feet (6 by 12 meters) with a flat tin roof. In the capital city of Mogadishu, most houses were painted white or a rosy beige. If an owner wanted to show that his living conditions had improved, he might build a new house of stone that he quarried in his spare time. Wood is scarce and is seldom used for buildings.

In 1970, 98 percent of houses in Mogadishu had neither water nor electricity. The government tried to cope with the rising tide of newcomers by tearing down shantytowns on the outskirts of cities and replacing them with more substantial housing. There

Somali women use their brightly colored futas to cover their heads, Islamic fashion (left). Nomadic men often use theirs wrapped as turbans around their heads (above).

were many difficulties, mainly lack of capital and qualified laborers who knew how to construct these buildings, but the government also found that the people often did not care for the newer style of architecture.

CLOTHING

The common dress for most Somali men and women is very much the same, regardless of where they come from. The *futa*, also called *maro* or *tob*, consists of 7 yards (6.4 meters) of cotton

A number of items are important to Somalis: (top left) the double-edged dagger of a nomad; (bottom left) the stick usually carried by a herdsman or farmer; and (right) the jewelry that is popular with both men and women.

wrapped sarong fashion around the body and tied at the waist. The Islamic dress code prescribes that the legs of both men and women must be covered. Herders often wrap a second futa around their heads to ward off heat. These futas are usually white, but after a few washings in muddy water, they are stained the color of the soil. Within cities, women are likely to wear colors. In most Islamic countries, women veil their faces, but not in Somalia.

Both women and men are fond of jewelry. Both sexes wear

A game of basketball brings out the need for modern, Western-style clothing for these girls at a city school.

necklaces and bracelets of gold, silver, and ivory. Many also wear amulets or charms, small leather bags with verses of the Qur'an, or Koran, inside, along with lions' claws, sharks' teeth, or some other object with supposedly magical power.

Nomads also wear a double-edged dagger in a sash belt. It is an all-round useful tool as well as a weapon. A typical stance of a herdsman is to rest his arms across a stick he carries on his shoulders. The stick is used to prod the animals along and also to sling any heavy items he might be carrying.

In the cities, Western dress has been adopted in offices. But Somalis often prefer the loose garments common to desert people.

FOOD

Hunger is a common affliction among Somalis. Little of the barren land is suitable for cultivation. However, the people of the different areas make do with what they can find.

A farm woman of the lower Shabeelle (above) makes porridge over her outdoor fire. The Italian influence has remained in the Somalis' liking for various kinds of pasta (right).

Among the northern nomads, milk is the principal food that sustains the young men who must travel with the camel herds. During the rainy season when the animals are at peak production, men may drink from 8 to 10 quarts (7.6 to 9.5 liters) of milk a day, supplemented with a bit of sorghum sweetener. The camels are usually not slaughtered unless an old one is nearing the end of its usefulness. This supplies meat perhaps no more than once or twice a month. Meat is served either boiled or cut in small slices and cooked in butter with aromatic herbs. It may also be dried in the sun and conserved in a vat of honey.

In the camp inhabited by the rest of the nomad family, food is more plentiful because they maintain their herds of sheep, goats, and some cattle. Sugar, durra (a type of grain sorghum with a slender stalk), rice, dates, and tea are also available.

Even among more settled, rural farmers, there is a limited diet, low in protein. They grow corn, durra, sorghum, beans, and a

Tea sellers in Kismaayo wait by the roadside for customers.

very limited amount of fruit and vegetables. Fish is available to those living near the coast, but it has never been a popular item of food for the Somalis. The government is trying to change tastes and to develop more efficient ways of harvesting the catch.

Millet and corn are staples. Millet is boiled in water to make a porridge. It can also be mixed with water and milk and made into cakes which are cooked over hot coals. Beans and squash are boiled or cooked with butter. Rice is the main staple, although it has to be imported.

People living in cities have a more balanced diet. However, the Food and Agriculture Organization of the United Nations has observed that although the average calorie intake is sufficient, Somali diets are low in protein and too high in fat and sugar. In the cities, European and Oriental food used to be available. One favorite holdover from Italian occupation is spaghetti or macaroni with a splash of sauce. The standard breakfast was once fried liver of sheep, goat, or camel, with onions and bread.

Some aspects of women's lives in Somalia (clockwise from top left): carrying water home, a perpetual task in this dry land; showing crafts in a market; acting in a traditional theatrical company; getting together with neighbors to work on needlework projects; shopping in a street market in Mogadishu.

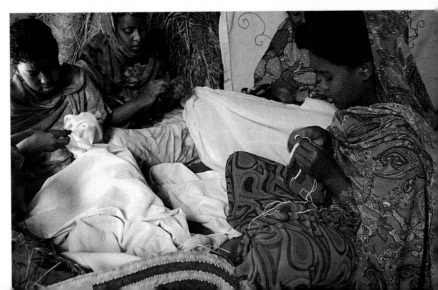

Before Mogadishu was mostly destroyed, its main market and bus terminal were located near each other.

MOGADISHU

Mogadishu is the country's capital, located on the Benadir coast. It was founded in the tenth century A.D. by Arab immigrants from the Persian Gulf. The city was at its height of influence and affluence in the thirteenth century.

Soon after, the Portuguese were attracted by the trade that occurred along that coast. Vasco da Gama bombarded the walls of the city from his ship, but he did not come ashore. Unlike the other Arab city-states farther south along the coast of East Africa, Mogadishu was never conquered by the Portuguese. It continued to be ruled by its own sultans until it accepted the overlordship of the Sultan of Oman in the nineteenth century.

When the Italians arrived in Mogadishu in the late 1880s, they established their own conclave of residents and over the next forty years built up their own European-style settlement.

The oldest mosque in Somalia, the Mosque of Sheik Abdul Aziz (right), survived the bombing of recent years. A legend among Somalis holds that the mosque rose fully built from the sea. The triangular Parliament House, shown above, suffered considerable damage.

Today the city has been bombed and looted. The buildings that remain range in age and style from the Mosque of Sheik Abdul Aziz, built in 1238, to the heavily damaged Parliament building constructed in the late 1960s. A museum houses some of the historical artifacts that have been saved. There is also an ornate Italian-constructed Roman Catholic cathedral that is a surprise in such a predominantly Muslim country.

The Hammawein is the original city of Mogadishu and was once one of the most beautiful sights on the east coast of Africa. The mosque of Fakr al-Din and the minaret of the Great Mosque are architectural masterpieces with elaborate decoration in Arabian style, of geometric design.

Today there are few tourists and no one to buy the carvings of

Mogadishu, after years of fighting, is a collection of contrasts between the beautiful old sections (left) and serious damage (right) that has taken away housing from the growing population.

ivory or meerschaum, a white clay-like substance often used in the bowls of pipes. White sand beaches that might once have attracted vacationers are left vacant until a lasting peace between warring clans can be promised.

NATURAL RESOURCES

Somalia has few natural resources other than its very limited agricultural produce. The most important mineral resource in use has been stone quarried for construction. Large quantities of lime-stone suitable for making cement are found near Berbera. Other non-metallic minerals of importance are gypsum-anhydrite, quartz sands suitable for the manufacture of glass, kaolin, and high-grade piezoquartz, used in electronics and optical instruments.

Ironworkers (left) will have deposits of iron ore to depend on in the future. Somalia's main resource is its agriculture. The women above are working in a factory where meat is canned for export.

Two large uranium deposits have been identified, although estimates of the grade of the ore vary. Iron-ore deposits were found in the Dhinsoor District of Bay Region, but the development of both iron and uranium will have to wait until there is a peaceful political solution. No foreign investors are willing to pledge funds for building up these industries until guarantees are given for a stable political base.

Sugar refineries were built in the 1970s with Italian capital, but all major production facilities have been taken over by the government. Other state-owned operations are a cigarette and match factory, a fruit- and vegetable-canning plant, meat- and fish-processing facilities, several grain mills, an iron foundry, and a petroleum refinery. Iraq furnished the funds for the oil refinery. There is a lack of managerial staff and skilled workers to carry on these enterprises.

A Somali Airline jet flies over a mosque in Mogadishu.

Somalia's basic sources of energy are domestic wood and charcoal, of which there is a limited supply. Petroleum must be imported, a fact that will make economic progress increasingly difficult for the country.

TRANSPORTATION

Transporting goods from one part of Somalia to another has always been a problem. There are surfaced roads between Mogadishu and Hargeysa. Elsewhere the roads are gravel or just tracks across the rough terrain. In the dry season, the unsealed roads and tracks are no problem, but when the rains come, ground transportation of any kind is bogged down.

There are still a number of boats plying up and down the coast, but few are suitable for passenger travel. Four main ports handle virtually all of the country's foreign trade. Port facilities at Berbera include two deep-water berths, one designed specifically for handling the movement of cattle.

There are two flights per week in either direction between Nairobi and Mogadishu, serviced by Kenya Airways and Somali

Airline. There are also two flights a week between Mogadishu and Berbera, a fine flight, some say, if you don't mind ex-air force pilots who still think they are flying MiG fighters.

RELIGION

Religion and family ties are the two most important factors that influence the lives of Somalis. The Islamic religion began in A.D. 622 with a man called Muhammad, who was born and grew up in the southwestern Arabia town of Mecca. Muhammad did not claim to be a holy person, only a prophet, but his teachings were held to be divinely inspired. People were told that anyone could talk to the God he called Allah. There were to be no churches or synagogues. According to the word of Allah, the wealthy were to provide for the poor. These were popular words for an impoverished people.

The basic teachings of Islam are recorded in the Qur'an, believed to have been given to Muhammad by God through the angel Gabriel. There were very specific rules that all the faithful must follow. Muslims must pray five times a day. Friday was to be their holy day. Certain foods were to be eaten, while others were forbidden.

The Qur'an, or Koran, of Islam is a well-used book for those Muslims who can read.

Discussions of the Qur'an and its teachings are an important
aspect of life for Muslim men.

There were periods of fasting. There were even rules as to how
women and men must dress. All local laws and government
rulings must be sanctioned by the religious community. There
was, indeed, no separation between everyday life and the holy life.
Each person was to submit to Allah. In fact, the name *Islam* means
"submission" in Arabic.

Before Islam reached the Somalis, quarrels over who would
follow Muhammad as the leader of the Muslims (or "those who
have submitted") had led to a split in the religious community.
There were the Sunnites, or traditionalists, and the Shiites, who
believed that only a direct descendant of the Prophet Muhammad
could be the rightful leader of Islam. All ethnic Somalis are
Sunnites.

In Islam there are no priests, but there are religious teachers,
preachers, and mosque officials. Religious training is obviously
more available in urban centers where children and adults alike

Women also study their religion in groups, though usually only with other women, not with men present.

learn to memorize parts of the Qur'an.

In some cases, a wandering teacher would set out to instruct a nomadic tribe, but if no "holy man" were available, a person of esteem was appointed to the position of *wadad*. This person might not have received formal training for his job, but he was entitled to lead prayers and to perform ritual sacrifices at weddings, on special holidays, and during festivals frequently held at the tombs of saints.

Somali Islam has developed certain religious orders that are recognized only within their own region. These are connected with the rise of Sufism, a mystical aspect of Islam that reached its height during the twelfth and thirteenth centuries. Sufism seeks a closer personal relationship to God through spiritual disciplines. Some sufis, or "holy men," become hermits to devote their life to prayer. The holy men were commonly called *dervishes*, a Persian word meaning someone who earns his livelihood by begging.

An old woodcut shows dervishes preparing for a ceremony in which music and whirling movements send them into a trance that allows them to be lifted into the presence of Allah.

These wandering dervishes often held spectacular ceremonies by going into trances brought on by group chanting, rhythmic gestures, dancing, and deep breathing. The object was to free oneself from the body and be lifted into the presence of God.

Most Somalis are nominally members of Sufi orders, but few undergo the rigors of complete dedication to the religious life. Membership in a brotherhood is theoretically a voluntary matter unrelated to kinship, yet more often than not, son will follow father into the father's order. There is a secret initiation when the novice swears to accept the head of the branch as his spiritual guide.

Somalis have modified much of Islam in terms of their own particular living situation. A leader is believed to have special powers to bless, and, in some cases, even to perform miracles, but his power may also bring disaster if he lays a curse on an individual or family.

The traditional education of a wadad includes a form of folk astronomy or astrology. It is he who predicts the best time for migration. He may also distribute charms to protect an individual.

In spite of Islam's belief that there is only one God, Somalis are apt to believe in the existence of mortal spirits, or *jinn*. Certain kinds of illnesses, including tuberculosis and pneumonia, are believed to be caused by spirit possession. This form of possession and the ceremony of exorcism used to treat it are sometimes called the "cult of zar."

Somalis, true to their Islamic tradition, do not drink alcohol. Instead, they often brew coffee beans that have been browned in butter, or tea that is steeped in cloves and cinnamon and sweetened with an enormous amount of sugar. The only stimulants often used are leaves of the qat plant, which contains a chemical related to the benzedrine family. When chewed, there is a mild intoxicating effect. It has been said that most Somali men are addicted to qat.

Although the Somali

This man in Baidoa is chewing qat leaves containing a mildly intoxicating substance.

government banned the sale of qat, it is readily available. Even during the period of war over the territory of Ogaden, the daily Air Somali qat flight from Dire Dawa to Mogadishu was always on time. Shooting at it by either side was out of the question.

RELIGION AND GOVERNMENT

As modern ways have encroached on even the most isolated clans, two opposite reactions have taken place in Somali religion. One response was to stress a return to orthodox Muslim tradition, completely opposing Westernization. Generally, the leaders of Islamic orders, fearing a weakening of their authority, tend to oppose Western education. Another response was to reform Islam by reinterpreting it in modern terms. Islamic socialism was the result.

The constitution of 1961 guaranteed freedom of religion, but it also declared the newly independent republic an Islamic state. The political coup of October 21, 1969, brought about deep-rooted change. The official declaration spelled out the differences between Islam and socialism. Islamic socialism, it was said, had become a servant of capitalism and a tool manipulated by a privileged, rich, and powerful class. Siad Barre, who became the leader after the coup, tried to replace the concept of Islamic socialism with the idea of scientific socialism, which he said had the same altruistic principles. However, it fit more closely with Soviet-style communism. According to Barre's scientific socialism, religious leaders were supposed to leave secular affairs to the new government. Those who attacked scientific socialism were seen as opposing Islam itself.

Above: A folksinger plays on a traditional sharero, *or Somalian guitar. Right: A co-educational class is held in the open under a tree. It was important to Somalia leaders in recent years that religion and education be emphasized.*

Religious leaders should exercise their moral influence but refrain from interfering with political or economic matters. Many who protested this logic were arrested, and some were killed.

EDUCATION

Until 1970, Somalia had no written language. The people possessed a splendid oral literary tradition exemplified by their highly stylized forms of poetry. Some of these older epics had been transcribed first into Arabic and later into Latin, but the Somalis possessed no recorded language of their own, not even an alphabet.

Left: Children learned to read and write Arabic to study the Qur'an in schools established in refugee camps. They used inks made of local plants to write on slates made of tree bark. Right: The Latin alphabet was the basis for the script that was developed for Somalia in the 1970s.

When the time came to develop a written language, some favored the Latin alphabet, but there was opposition from religious leaders who argued that a "Christian" script was unsuitable for a Muslim country. English and Italian were languages used by some of the more educated people who had been officials during colonial rule by these two countries, but the ruling government of Somalia viewed the official use of foreign languages as a threat to national unity. It was also true that only a very small percentage of the people knew either of these languages. The result would be to further divide the society on the basis of education.

In a school established by UN peacekeepers in 1993, little girls are learning the Brambur, a traditional Somali dance.

Arabic was perhaps the most widely used second language, but past conflicts with their Arab-speaking neighbors brought opposition to that suggestion. Finally a modified version of Latin was adopted as the standard script. All government officials were given three months to learn the new script and become proficient in its use. The deadline was later extended to six months. By 1973, schoolbooks were being produced in the new writing.

Somali's literacy rate was estimated at only 5 percent in 1972. After adopting the new script, the government set out on a crash program to bring about a "cultural revolution" aimed at making the entire population literate in two years.

The first campaign was started in the cities and settled areas. More than 20,000 teachers were needed. Half of them came from teenage students whose own classes were suspended while they spread out over the countryside to teach others the skills of reading and writing the simplest of texts. The rural program compelled privileged young people to share the hardships of life with nomads, which gave each class a more sympathetic view of the other's way of life. However, the literacy rate in Somalia is still probably only about 25 percent.

The Somali National University offered college-level courses in law, economics, social studies, Islamic studies, and statistics. Its graduates were given two years' credit toward a university degree at Italian universities. The university was virtually destroyed in the civil war of the early 1990s.

HEALTH

Somalia is one of the poorest countries in the world, and it has one of the most discouraging health records. The average life expectancy, even before the civil wars of the 1990s, was estimated

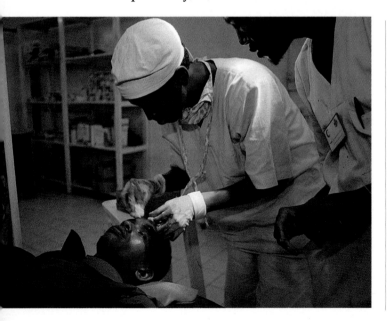

A Somali doctor at work in Kisenyi Hospital in northern Mogadishu works on the eyes of a patient. Blindness is often caused by one of the many eye infections rampant in Somalia.

Women visit a laboratory in the outpatient clinic of one of the few hospitals in Somalia.

at forty-one years, and 177 out of every 1,000 babies die at birth. It is believed that at least two-thirds of these deaths could be avoided by simple preventive measures. But lack of roads and a largely mobile population make it hard for the government to bring health care to rural areas.

As early as 1972, the government took control of medical services. Patients were admitted to hospitals without cost to the patients. That same year, the government took over the importation of all drug products, which were made available to citizens at reasonable cost. It was a step in the right direction, but without sufficient funds to modernize the medical care, the people suffered.

The lack of safe water and waste-disposal facilities and the difficulty of preserving food without refrigeration are the causes of many intestinal diseases. Tuberculosis and malaria and other parasitic diseases are major problems. In addition, tetanus, venereal disease, leprosy, heart disease, and poliomyelitis, which could be controlled by vaccination, are prevalent. A variety of eye

There are no tourists to enjoy this coastal beach, only a bird and a man praying.

infections have caused blindness in many people.

In the 1970s, the World Health Organization began a major tuberculosis-control plan in Somali cities. The project's aim was to vaccinate the entire population. This task turned out to be impossible to carry out among the semi-nomadic population.

During the rainy season, all Somalis are exposed to malaria. The larvae of the disease-carrying mosquito are transported from well to well in nomads' water skins. Water tanks built to store water collected during the rainy season have turned into hazardous breeding grounds for the mosquito.

In some parts of the marshy river areas in the south, most of the inhabitants are affected by intestinal parasites. Weakened by the parasites, they are susceptible to a score of other afflictions. Malnutrition has decreased their chances of recovery.

Somalia's leaders were working on increasing educational, economic, and health opportunities for the people when a change in government threw the nation into anarchy. It may take decades for the country to recover from the chaos.

Chapter 7

INDEPENDENCE

The Trust Territory of Somaliland established in 1950 under Italian administration had the advantage that a definite date had been set for independence. There was no such deadline for British Somaliland, which was eventually to be merged with the trust territory.

A territorial council was set up in 1950 to serve as the base for the country's future self-government. It engaged in full-scale debate concerning proposed legislation to run the country. The district councils responsible for rural areas were considerably weaker than their urban counterparts as a natural result of the pastoral economy. The

Somalis celebrated the independence of their country in 1960 by parading in the streets of Mogadishu. In the background is the Roman Catholic cathedral, one of the few Christian churches in this Islamic nation.

Somalis proudly hold up their flag during a demonstration organized by supporters of General Aidid.

rural councils were primarily engaged with settling disputes over grazing and water rights.

Finally, in April 1960, the British government agreed to release British Somaliland so that it could unite with the Italian Trust Territory on the date when this part of the country was to legally gain its freedom. Leaders of the two territories met in Mogadishu to set the wheels of a unified government rolling.

A constitution was drawn up whereby the country was to be ruled by a president elected as head of state. A parliamentary form of government responsible to a democratically elected national legislature was set up. The legislature was initially composed of the 123 members of the two territorial assemblies.

A NEW NATION

On July 1, 1960, the independent Somali Republic was officially inaugurated. The legislature's appointment of Abdirashid Ali Shermarke to the presidency of the republic was confirmed in a national referendum the following year. The son of the inventor of the Osmaniya script used in producing the country's first written literature, he had been one of the founders of the Somali Youth League in 1943.

During the early years of independence, Somalia enjoyed democracy. It mirrored the Somali code, giving every man the right to be heard. There were many who took advantage of this right. Politics became a favorite occupation. A radio was the most desired possession, not for entertainment but to keep abreast of political news. Some observers felt that the future of Somalia suffered from an overabundance of democracy. With too many

Abdirashid Ali Shermarke, the first president of Somalia, was assassinated in 1969.

voices, there was lack of direction.

Although officially unified, the Italian Trust Territory in the south and the former British Protectorate in the north were actually governed separately. Italy and Britain had left the country with two separate administrative, legal, and educational systems, conducted in different languages. Police, taxes, and the exchange rates of their separate currencies were also different.

From the beginning, there was dissatisfaction with the distribution of power among the clan families. Those in the north felt they were not given a representative share of the power.

The most important political issue in Somali politics was the unification of all areas populated by Somali people into one country, a concept know as pan-Somalism. The exact size of the National Assembly was not established, so as to permit the inclusion of future representatives of the contested areas after the hoped-for unification.

The national flag is a white five-pointed star on a blue field. The points are said to represent those areas claimed as part of the Somali nation: the former Italian and British territories, Ogaden in Ethiopia, Djibouti, and the Northern Frontier District (NFD) in Kenya. The Somalis did not outright claim sovereignty over adjacent territory, but rather demanded that Somalis living there be granted the right of self-determination.

This obviously was not approved by the governments of Kenya or Ethiopia. Hostilities at both borders grew in intensity. There were almost daily clashes. Finally in February 1964, a cease-fire was established under the auspices of the Organization of African Unity (OAU), but fear of additional conflicts was not eased.

Although Somali leaders were on friendly terms with Western powers, particularly Britain and Italy, they also established close ties with both the Soviet Union and China. The Soviet Union had been helpful in providing loans to finance the training and equipping of the armed forces. During the 1960s, more than eight hundred Somalis received military training in the Soviet Union. Somalis, on the other hand, resented the large-scale military aid given by the United States to neighboring Ethiopia.

During this decade, there was a continual reshuffling of party power. In 1967, President Shermarke nominated Mohamed Ibrahim Egal (also written *Igaal*) as prime minister. The new man was known to take a more moderate position on pan-Somali issues. He was in favor of improving relations with other African countries. However, official corruption was spreading on a

Mohamed Ibrahim Egal (left) was named prime minister by President Shermarke in 1967. Here he stands with U.S. President Lyndon Johnson at the funeral of the assassinated Shermarke.

large scale. Among the most dissatisfied were intellectuals and members of the armed forces and police.

A SOCIALIST GOVERNMENT

The stage was set for a coup d'état, a sudden overthrow of the government. On October 15, 1969, Shermarke was killed by a member of his own bodyguard. Another person from the Darod clan-family was nominated for president but was not confirmed. Many believed that the same corrupt policies would continue without drastic action.

Early in the morning of October 21, 1969, the army took over the country, led by General Muhammed Siad Barre, who claimed the presidency for himself. He set up a Supreme Revolutionary Council (SRC), composed of two dozen military officers. What infuriated his opponents was that he packed the government with members of his own clan, the Marehan, a small group making up only 1 percent of the country's population.

Democracy came to an end, and the country's freely elected National Assembly was abolished. Important rights, such as freedom of speech, were limited. Many of Siad Barre's opponents were arrested, and some were executed. Political parties were banned, and the constitution suspended. The new government vowed to end tribalism, nepotism, corruption, and misrule. A major goal was Somali unification. The country's name was changed from the Somali Republic to the Somali Democratic Republic (SDR), and it was declared a socialist state.

The new government's policies were guided by the teachings of the Qur'an and a type of "scientific socialism" that had been

Huge posters showing General Muhammed Siad Barre lined the streets of Mogadishu for many years.

adopted from Soviet-style communism. The system of local government was broken down into smaller units to help destroy the influence of the traditional clan assemblies. The headmen, who had been recognized as representatives of their groups, were replaced by dignitaries known as peacemakers, *nabod doan,* appointed directly by the SDR.

Crash programs were set up to improve economic and social development. A Somali language in a standard written form was adopted to put laws in official form. A twenty-five-member military junta was set up to rule the country. Theoretically, actions to be taken were to be decided by a majority vote of this select body. In reality, President Siad Barre was the man who influenced these decisions. Top civilian district and regional officials were replaced by military officers. The few remaining civil servants were required to attend reorientation courses that combined professional training with political indoctrination.

Siad Barre proved to be adept at getting his way. He controlled what was written about him and what went out over the radio waves. The image he wished to project was as a savior of his people. The press referred to him as "Victorious Leader" (*Guulwaadde*). Portraits of him displayed beside portraits of Marx and Lenin festooned the streets on public occasions. For some Somalis, who had always looked up to the leading warrior of a clan, Barre took on this image.

Despite his claimed intention to do away with clan-families, Barre chose as his inner circle only those who were intimately related to his family. President Barre's own son-in-law, Colonel Ahmed Suleiman Abdulle, was one of the five military officers who ran the country.

To help some of the starving population, the new regime, with Soviet help, resettled some 140,000 nomads in farming communities or coastal towns. In some cases, this improved their living conditions, but not all were happy. By moving, the nomads had severed their clans' ties to specific areas of land. Also, the government's attempts to improve the status of Somali women were blocked by traditionalists who adhered to Islamic teachings.

Setting up a socialist government was difficult. Foreign capital was needed, but foreign intervention of any kind was outlawed by the Somali legislature. In some cases, private business was allowed, but by 1970, Italian- and British-owned banks and petroleum companies operating in Somalia were brought under government control. The state also took over the distribution and pricing of domestic goods, such as sugar, to keep prices in line.

Somalia's traditional problem of drought brought further problems. The drought of 1975-76 was the worst in memory. The

Drought and the subsequent famine that killed many Somali people forced Barre to change his focus from development to relief in the 1970s.

government was forced to divert funds intended for development projects to meet the needs of at least 200,000 refugees rounded up in relief centers.

At the time of the coup, Somalia was listed by the United Nations as one of the world's least developed countries. Somalia finally had to beg for foreign assistance just to meet basic needs. When the Soviets offered support, the Somalis gladly took it. The Soviets developed a naval base on Somalia's Indian Ocean coast and also sent military equipment, which would soon be used in aggressive attacks against Somali neighbors.

Somalia joined the Arab League in 1974, hoping for support in its claim to recover "lost territories" in the Ogaden. Somali guerrillas attacked bases within Ethiopia, successfully cutting railroad bridges between Addis Ababa and Djibouti. But suddenly there was a shift of power. On September 12, 1974, the long-time emperor of Ethiopia, Haile Selassie, was removed from power by a military group aided by Soviet equipment and officers. The Soviets gradually developed ties to the new socialist government in

An anti-Soviet poster showed the Communists bombing unarmed citizens. The Soviets were thrown out of Somalia after they helped Ethiopia defeat Somali troops.

Ethiopia. This was resented in Somalia. In 1977, when Somalia invaded the Ogaden, the Soviets supported the Ethiopians. In November, Somalia retaliated by expelling all Soviet advisors.

In 1978 Somali soldiers were driven back by a large force of Soviet-backed Ethiopians. Somalia turned elsewhere for help. The United States decided to defend Somalia in return for the use of seaports and airfields guarding the Gulf of Aden and the route to the Suez Canal. Again, strange partners and treaties brought about a temporary balance of power in the region, but it was not a healthy or thriving region.

CIVIL WAR

The Siad Barre government, aware of its own birth by military force, spent most of its political skill in maintaining its grip on power, rather than on achieving the social reforms they had promised from the outset. Anyone speaking out against the government was jailed. According to a former official, many, if not most, influential Somalis had been jailed at least once.

Frustrated at its failure to defeat guerrilla rebels of the Somali National Movement (SNM), the army turned to indiscriminate bombing and shelling of areas containing civilians suspected of sympathizing with the guerrillas. Land mines were laid across wide areas. Water reservoirs and livestock were destroyed. Members of the Isaq clan, the major ethnic group of northern Somalia, were systematically persecuted. The fighting forced nearly half a million Somalis to leave the country, most of them becoming refugees in Ethiopia.

The brutality of the Barre regime increased the opposition to Barre. Barre responded by viciously suppressing members of several clan-families. Statistics leaked to concerned international human-rights groups, such as the U.S.-based Africa Watch, were worse than anyone imagined. In northern Somalia alone, an estimated 50,000 to 60,000 civilians were killed within a two-year period. The major city of Hargeysa was left in rubble.

Government atrocities were also reported spreading to central and southern Somalia. Two large clans formed their own political movements to oppose Barre. The country was in a state of anarchy.

On July 6, 1990, Siad Barre's bodyguards killed at least sixty-five people at a soccer match, opening fire when spectators booed

Troops of the United Somali Congress, which was headed by Muhammad Ali Mahdi, keep watch from a mosque tower, or minaret, in Mogadishu during the height of the takeover in 1990.

and threw stones at Barre, who was making a pre-game speech. One week later, the government ordered forty-six prominent Somalis to stand trial after they had signed a manifesto calling for free elections and an improvement in human rights. Charges were finally dropped, but the atmosphere of suspicion and retribution was causing chaos throughout the country.

President Barre called a meeting to fire his old cabinet after accusing its members of failing to solve the country's dire political and economic problems. Barre's opponents, however, knew that Barre had been the one in complete control. Now his own army and his political friends were deserting him. Rebel groups were massing for an attack. It was said that the unpaid soldiers of Somalia's official army routinely raised money by kidnapping shopkeepers. No one was trusted.

Both U.S. and Italian forces began separate air and sea operations to rescue foreigners from Mogadishu. Earlier attempts to evacuate foreigners had been hindered by the rebel groups' unwillingness to interrupt the fighting.

Those Somalis who had fled across the border to Ethiopia

Children were caught in the growing problems of drought, famine, civil war, and the total instability of the country.

found themselves caught in the crossfire of a civil war in that country as well. Death and starvation met them at every turn. United Nations food relief was frequently confiscated by the Ethiopian army. There was no food or clean water in the refugee camps and only limited health care.

In December 1990, the United Somali Congress (basically the Hawiye clan-family) hit the capital of Mogadishu. In the bloody street fighting, Siad Barre's prized troops, the Red Berets, were unable to defend their positions. On New Year's Eve, Siad Barre escaped from Somalia and eventually sought refuge in Nigeria.

Muhammad Ali Mahdi, head of the USC, became president. He gave a promise to hold open elections at the end of two years.

Before the new government could be organized, there was a

split in leadership. Ali Mahdi belonged to the Abgals subclan of the Hawiye. Another subclan, the Habir Gesdir, was led by General Muhammad Farah Aidid. The followers of these two most powerful warlords in the country could not agree to cooperate in forming a centralized government.

Barre was gone, but the situation was still desperate. There was no food. People had been driven off their farms and grazing land. When they headed for the few urban centers, there was no place for them to live. Lack of sanitation and famine took the lives of thousands. The news of Somalia's plight gradually reached the outside world. The enormity of the problem surprised even those who had warned of the distressing conditions.

OPERATION RESTORE HOPE

The International Red Cross and its Islamic counterpart, the Red Crescent, mounted a relief effort to help the starving Somalis. Other agencies, such as the United Nations World Food Program, CARE, and the Save the Children Service, organized convoys of supplies to be sent.

Unfortunately, organized gangs of bandits stole the food and medical supplies as fast as they were unloaded from ships and truck convoys. Gasoline was shipped into the port of Berbera to service trucks that were delivering supplies. The government said that it was needed for military tanks instead. Corn and grain were shipped in, but the government would not let them be unloaded without a huge dockage charge. As a result, some supplies were sent to Mozambique where there was also a need for relief. Money spent by the United Nations in Aidid's territory to the north fueled

Though aid was sent to Somalia from around the world, the food stored in warehouses was often stolen and sold before it could be distributed.

the conflict by providing his supporters with arms to fight his rival, Ali Mahdi.

It was obvious that the international relief efforts were not helping the people most in need. In December 1992, a Red Cross worker was fatally shot as he tried to hand out food in Mogadishu. The same day, sixty tons of food in the Red Cross warehouse were stolen. In the Mogadishu market, guns were sold like groceries.

The patience of the world came to an end. It was time for more forceful measures. However, the United States did not want to send troops. They had just fought a war with Iraq and were helping the Kurds, who had been persecuted under the Iraqi government. They were also being asked to quell a civil war in Yugoslavia. It was left to the United Nations forces to provide protection for relief workers.

In 1992 when Boutros Boutros-Ghali became secretary-general

Warlords Aidid (left) and Mahdi (right) shook hands in a truce arranged in December 1992 by the secretary-general of the United Nations. However, the fighting continued as soldiers of Operation Restore Hope landed.

of the United Nations, he arranged a truce with the two strongmen in Somalia—Aidid and Mahdi. In April the UN Security Council voted to send fifty unarmed military observers from Pakistan to Somalia. However, fighting and looting continued. The peacekeeping group was there only to monitor the truce. It had no power to enforce punishment for violators. Countries of Africa criticized the United Nations for sending 14,000 peacekeepers to Yugoslavia and only a token force to Somalia. Pictures of the worsening conditions in refugee camps finally brought action.

Between 1991 and mid-1993, an estimated 250,000 to 300,000 Somalis died from the fighting or from famine, according to UN estimates. Once the West and the United Nations swung into action with a relief airlift in the months from August to December 1992, 100,000 to 125,000 lives were saved, the report says. But no political solution was forthcoming. The fighting did not stop.

On June 5, 1993, twenty-five Pakistani soldiers were killed in

Women carry home food distributed by forces from Saudi Arabia (above). Italian troops, shown at right raising their flag, arrived in Somalia for the first time in decades.

an ambush. The UN immediately passed a resolution to go after the culprits and punish them. Senior UN officials named Aidid as the master of the terrorists. He denied it.

Armed troops from the United States and other countries arrived. On July 12, 1993, UN troops bombed without warning what they thought was an Aidid command post. An estimated fifty people were killed but not their leader. The mistake, many analysts said later, was that instead of going after Aidid's militia, the UN troops went after Aidid himself. This meant that the United Nations could no longer be regarded as a neutral force.

On October 3, 1993, Aidid's forces killed eighteen U.S. Rangers, and at least two hundred Somalis in battle. Four days later, U.S. President Bill Clinton announced that he was ordering United States troops out of Somalia by March 1, 1994.

The day the U.S. forces landed on the beaches of Somalia they

A United States Marine carries food supplies for a child in Baidoa.

were greeted by television cameras and smiling, welcoming Somalis. Twenty-seven months later, 7,000 United States troops returned to Somalia's coast to protect the exit of the last Pakistani and Bangladeshi UN peacekeeping troops from the country.

Instead of friendly faces lining the beaches, heavily armed vehicles with Somali machine-gun crews waited outside the port and airport to seize every bit of property the departing troops abandoned. Operation Restore Hope had saved lives, but it had not created any kind of a lasting peace.

It was said that instead of focusing primarily on the two warlords, the United Nations should have worked more with national leaders, businessmen, and intellectuals in various parts of the country, who knew the problems—and the clans—at first-hand. The key issue during 1993 and 1994, which was still not settled by 1996, is the ownership of farmland and grazing land in southern and central Somalia. The country's internal wars are the result of centuries-old movements of major Somali clans south

A boy holds seeds he was given as part of an international project to revive agriculture in wartorn Somalia.

from the nomadic grazing areas that have become over-populated. The death toll may have temporarily eased the problem, but too many displaced Somalis want to return to the land they believe to be their birthright.

SIGNS OF PROGRESS

Nature may have brought about the first signs of healing. In August and September of 1995, farmers had a good harvest. In the area between the Jubba and Shabeelle rivers in central Somalia, some farmers returned home, after fleeing earlier violence.

Of approximately fifty-eight district councils (local governments) formed with the encouragement of the United Nations, forty-five continued to function. True, they are struggling and still may not survive without greater regional taxation or outside assistance, but there is a show of cooperation. Even in divided Mogadishu, changes have come about.

Peace is hard to come by because the individual clans are still seeking to grab all the power they can, regardless of the needs of the country. No clan seems ready to trust another, at least until there has been a time of healing.

Foreign troops have pulled out, but such international assistance agencies as CARE have stayed on to train health workers, restore important water reservoirs near Baidoa, and give advice for agricultural projects. There are predictions that there will be more fighting, but after the UN pullout, Somalis realized that there's no more international rescue ahead. Perhaps they will reach their own solution, one that can become firmer with each passing generation.

Somalia has hope for the future if its leaders will concentrate on the people instead of on war and the power of the clans.

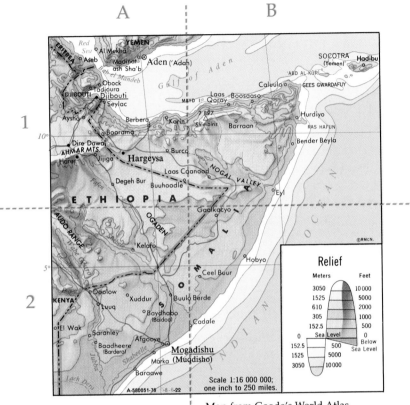

Map from Goode's World Atlas,
© Rand McNally, R.L. 96-S-125

SOMALIA

MINI-FACTS AT A GLANCE

GENERAL INFORMATION

Official Name: Soomaaliya (Somali), Somalia.

Capital: Mogadishu.

Government: Somalia was ruled by a military group, the Supreme Revolutionary Council, from 1969 till 1991 when the government was overthrown by the United Somali Congress (USC) rebels. A president and cabinet were appointed to run the country, but soon factions developed within the USC, and warlords and their supporters took control of different parts of the country. Militia and armed gangs have controlled the nation since the fall of government in 1991. Several groups seem to be preparing to set up their own government, but as of mid- 1996, there is no effective national or local government. According to the 1979 constitution, the country is to be run by a president elected as head of state, with the National Assembly as the legislative organ. The judicial system is largely based on Islamic laws. For administrative purposes, the country is divided into sixteen regions.

Religion: Islam is the official religion. The largest group is the Sunni Muslim with 99.5 percent of the population, followed by Christians with 0.1 percent, and others with 0.4 percent.

Ethnic Composition: Almost 98 percent of the population is of Somali stock; followed by Arab, 1 percent; and Bantu and others, 1 percent. The Somalis are divided into six major clan-families, tracing their origin to two brothers, Samaal and Saab; four families—Dir, Darod, Isaq, and Hawiye—are descendants of Samaal and are predominantly pastoral; the other two —Digil and Rahanweyn —trace their origin to Saab and are agricultural.

Language: Somali and Arabic are the official languages. English and Italian are also spoken. A new Somali script, introduced in 1972, has been one of the nation's strongest unifying factors.

National Flag: The design of the Somali flag is based on the flag of the United Nations as Somalia was once a UN Trust Territory. The national flag has a white five-pointed star on a blue field. The points of the star are said to represent those areas claimed as part of the Somali nation—the former Italian and British territories, Ogaden (Ethiopia), Djibouti, and the Northern Frontier District (NFD) in Kenya.

National Emblem: A light-blue shield with a gold border displays a large five-pointed white star in the center; black-spotted African leopards hold the sides of the shield with their paws.

National Anthem: "Somalia Hanolato" ("Long Live Somalia").

National Calendar: Gregorian and Islamic.

Money: Somali shilling (So. Sh.) is the official currency. In early 1996, 2,620 Somali shillings were equal to U.S. $1.

Membership in International Organizations: African, Caribbean, and Pacific Countries (ACP); African Development Bank (AfDB); Arab League (AL); Islamic League (IL); Arab Monetary Fund (AMF); Economic Commission of Africa (ECA); International Organization for Migration (IOM); Islamic Development Bank (IDB); Non-aligned Movement (NAM); Organization of African Unity (OAU), Qrganization of the Islamic Conference (OIC); United Nations (UN).

Weights and Measures: The metric system is in use.

Population: 7,233,000 (1995 estimates; excludes some 600,000 Somali refugees in neighboring countries); 27.1 persons per sq. mi. (10.5 persons per sq km), with 37 percent living in towns and 63 percent, primarily nomadic, living in rural areas.

Cities:

    Mogadishu 1,000,000*
    Hargeysa 90,000
    Kismaayo 86,000
    Berbera 83,000
    Marka 60,000**
    (Based on 1984 estimates; *1990; **1981)

GEOGRAPHY

Border: Located on the Horn of Africa, the most easterly part of the continent, Somalia is bordered on the north by the Gulf of Aden, on the east by the Indian Ocean, on the west by Kenya and Ethiopia, and on the northwest by Djibouti. Somalia has not finally accepted its international boundaries with any of its neighboring countries.

Coastline: 1,839 mi. (2,960 km).

Land: The physiography of Somalia has little variation. The scrub-covered, semi-arid Guban Plain extends parallel to the Gulf of Aden in the north. These dry plains rise through a series of hills to the Ogo plateau region characterized by shallow and dry river valleys. Extending from the northeast to the central part, the plateau merges with the Mudug Plain in south-central Somalia. The cooler and drier Haud plateau region in the south has thorn-bush and tall grasses. The Golis and Ogo mountains with their steep escarpments, dominate the Somali landscape. The Nugaal (or Nogal) Valley region along the Indian Ocean coast is the traditional home of pastoral nomads. The Shabeelle and Jubba river region in the south is the most important agricultural region.

Highest Point: Mount Surud Ad, 7,900 ft. (2,408 m).

Lowest Point: Sea level.

Rivers: There are only two permanent rivers—the Jubba and the Shabeelle—both originating in the Ethiopian Highlands. They provide water for irrigation and are navigable by large vessels for short distances only. The 1,250-mi. (2,011-km)-long Shabeelle, or "Leopard," River disappears in a series of marshes and sand flats before reaching the Indian Ocean. The Jubba River flows from the Ethiopian Highlands to the Indian Ocean, and is navigable by shallow-draft vessels. Both rivers are lined with narrow borders of forests.

Forests: Less than 15 percent of the area is forested. Forests in the north produce frankincense and myrrh, which are important Somali exports. The government has trial-planted teak, gmelina, mahogany, and eucalyptus with limited success. Forest products include acacia, thorntree, aloes, baobab, candelabra, mangrove, papaya, and kapok. Most of the trees are cut down to be used as firewood.

Wildlife: Even after decades of illegal hunting and poaching, there are still a large variety of game and wild animals left in Somalia including antelope, leopard, cheetah, buffalo, zebra, hippopotamus, dugong (similar to a manatee), elephant, rhinoceros, giraffe, gazelle, dik-dik (a small antelope), kudu, lion, and wild donkey. Poisonous snakes, pythons, monitor lizards, large sea turtles, and crocodiles are also common. Monkeys and warthogs cause a lot of damage to agricultural areas. Almost 450 different species of birds live in or pass through Somalia, including ducks, geese, pelicans, herons, flamingos, cormorants, eagles, vultures, owls, hawks, grouse, bustards, and ostriches.

Climate: The tropical climate has very little seasonal change in temperatures. Most of Somalia has four seasons, two dry and two with only a small amount of rain. Hot, dry, and dusty winds are prevalent in December-March or *jilal* season; *gu* season lasts from March to May and brings the country's heaviest rains; *hagaa* season, with frequent dust storms, starts in June and continues through August; the second wet season, *dayr*, lasts from September through December and accounts for 30 percent of annual rainfall. Rain falls in two seasons and is influenced by the seasonal monsoon winds. Most of the country receives less than 20 in. (50 cm) of rainfall annually; it decreases from south to north. Droughts are common. The northeast coast is extremely hot during the summer with average temperatures of 95° to 100° F. (35° to 38° C). The mean daily maximum temperatures range from 86° to 104° F. (30° to 40° C).

Greatest Distance: North to South: 950 mi. (1,529 km).
                           East to West: 730 mi. (1,175 km).
Area: 246,200 sq. mi. (637,650 sq km).

ECONOMY AND INDUSTRY

Agriculture: Less than 5 percent of the total land is available for cultivation, but almost 20 percent of the workforce is engaged in agricultural activities. During the Italian occupation, Italians introduced banana farming on large-scale plantations in the southern region. Bananas, sugarcane, citrus fruits, papaya, kapok, and cotton are the chief crops. Irrigation is available in the river valleys of the southern region. Natural depressions sometimes fill with water in rainy season and are used as temporary ponds for irrigation.

Fishing is not popular because Somalis dislike eating fish, but there is an ample supply of anchovies, sardines, herring, tuna, flounder, grouper, snappers, and mackerel. Government has sponsored several projects to encourage the Somali fishing industry.

Livestock: Nearly three-fourths of the Somali population is pastoral and is engaged in livestock-raising. With some 50 percent of the land under pasture and grassland, livestock-raising is the most important economic activity, and contributes about one-half of the total exports. Somali nomads wander endlessly in search of grass and water for their animals. In the western part of the country, herders and farmers have dug wells in areas where a limited water supply is just below the surface of the ground; the nomads return to these wells in the dry season.

Mining: Somalia's mineral resources are few and include limestone, gypsum-anhydrite, salt, zinc, copper, manganese quartz sands (for glass), kaolin, high grade piezoquartz (used in electronics and optical instruments), and some uranium. Deposits of petroleum and natural gas remain unexploited because of an unstable political situation. Energy is produced from domestic wood, charcoal, and imported petroleum.

Manufacturing: The manufacturing sector is small and most of the industrial establishments are owned by the government. Somalia has a cigarette and match factory, a fruit- and vegetable-canning plant, a meat- and fish-processing plant, several grain mills, an iron foundry, and a petroleum refinery. Some handicrafts, such as leather bags and dagger pouches, are common.

Transportation: Transportion of goods has always been a problem in Somalia as the few roads connect only major cities. There are no railroads. In the early 1990s, there were 13,500 mi. (21,700 km) of roads of which one-third were paved. Buses and trucks are the major means of transportation in the interior. Goods are carried by boats along the Indian Ocean and Gulf of Aden coast. Although Somalia has a long coastline, there is only one major port, Berbera; it has two deep-water berths, one specifically for handling cattle. Somali Airline is the national carrier; Mogadishu and Berbera are the two major airports.

Communication: All communication media are controlled by the government. In 1993 there was one daily newspaper published in Somalia (circulation data are not reliable). In the early 1990s, there was one radio receiver per 16 persons, one television set per 2,000 persons, and one telephone per 700 persons.

Trade: Chief imports are rice and other cereals, petroleum, paper, cement, steel, machinery, and textiles. Major import sources are Italy, the Netherlands, Bahrain, United Kingdom, Djibouti, China, Germany, and Thailand. Chief export items are live animals (sheep, goats, and camels), animal hides and skins, bananas, papaya, and fish and fish products. Major export destinations are Italy, Saudi Arabia, Yemen, and United Arab Emirates.

EVERYDAY LIFE

Health: The nation's few health facilities are concentrated in Mogadishu and few other cities; government dispensaries serve the rural areas. Major diseases are leprosy, eye problems, malaria, tetanus, and tuberculosis. Many intestinal diseases are caused by lack of safe drinking water and safe waste-disposal and refrigeration facilities. Life expectancy of 45 years for males and 49 years for females is among the lowest in the world. The infant-mortality rate of 122 per 1,000 live births is among the highest in the world. In the late 1980s, there were some 19,000 persons per physician and 1,000 persons per hospital bed. With civil wars and famines, malnutrition has become one of the major causes of death.

Education: All schools are under government control and there are no private schools. Although education is provided free of charge, very few children go to school, especially in rural areas. Primary education lasts for eight years and is oflicially compulsory for children aged 6 to 14 years. A modified version of Latin was adopted as Somalia's first standard script in 1970, and soon all school and college textbooks were being produced in the Somali language. The Somali National University at Mogadishu used to offer courses in law, economics, social studies, Islamic studies, and statistics; it was closed in 1991 and the building was severely damaged during the civil war. There are a few vocational and technical schools in large cities. Somalia's literacy rate was about 5 percent in 1972, but with government efforts it rose to almost 25 percent by the early 1990s—still one of the lowest in the world.

Holidays:

New Year's Day, January 1
Labor Day, May 1
Independence Day, June 26
Foundation of the Republic, July 1

The Islamic holidays, such as Id al-Fitr, Id al-Adha, Ashoura, and Mouloud, are dependent on the Islamic lunar calendar and vary from year to year.

Culture: Poetry reading is an essential part of the Somali culture. Poetry subjects range from war, peace, and family to horses and camels. Because they had no written language, Somalis developed a rich oral literature. Most of the buildings of architectural importance are in Mogadishu, such as the mosques of Sheik Abdul Aziz and Fakr al-Din, the National Museum, and the National Theater.

Social: Traditionally Somali social and political organizations have been based on kinship groups. Clans are as large as 100,000 people strong, and are still the largest political units with ceremonial heads known as *soldaan*. There are thousands of personal family lineage groups, and Somalis strictly follow their kinship rules.

The Samaal clan-families roam in the area west of the Jubba River where pasture supports camels, sheep, and goats. Samaal clans are associated with a given territory, defined by a customary path of migration and not by specific boundaries. The *shir* is an assembly of adult Samaal males who carry out clan rules. The Saab clans live in the area between the Shabeelle and Jubba rivers and raise cattle and grow crops. Saab clan affairs are handled by leading elders called *gobwein*. There is often harsh fighting between the clans over the possession of water sources.

The religious teachers, preachers, and mosque officials play an important role in the Somali society; they teach children and adults alike to memorize parts of the Qur'an. A religious leader is believed to have special power to bless, to perform miracles, and to distribute protective charms to an individual or a family. Women have generally been made subordinate to men, but because of civil war and famine, a growing number of female-headed households have emerged.

Family: Samaal marriage is not only a religious ceremony, but also a contract of economic and political importance. Marriage within a lineage group is forbidden; bride and groom have to be separated by at least six or more generations.

A wife never really becomes a member of her husband's lineage, but her children belong to her husband's lineage. Saab people typically marry within their group, and a Saab man prefers to marry his father's brother's daughter.

Dress: The Somali dress for both men and women is very much the same. They both wear the *futa*, which is a 7-yard (6.4-m) piece of cloth wrapped toga fashion around the body and tied at the waist. A second futa is wrapped around the head to ward off heat. Both men and women are fond of jewelry and wear necklaces and bracelets of gold, silver, and ivory. Nomads carry a double-edged dagger in a sash belt. Men like to keep their hair long and bushy till they get married; women and girls braid their hair in narrow rows. Western dress has largely been adopted in the cities.

Housing: Nomads have portable elongated tents, called *agal,* which can be easily taken to pieces and transported by camel. Bundles of weeds or poles are used to build the frame. The bed is made of woven palm-leaf ribs supported by four wooden stacks. In settled villages, people live in clusters of houses with mud walls and thatched roofs; a *muudul* is a circular hut and an *arish* is a rectangular hut. Arab-style houses are built one or two stories high with flat roofs. There is an acute shortage of housing in the cities.

Food: Milk, millet, and corn are staples for Somalis. Meat is generally eaten only once or twice a month, either boiled or cut in small slices and cooked in butter with aromatic herbs. In the pastoral villages, sugar, sorghum, rice, dates, beans, and tea are part of the meal; very little fresh fruit and vegetables are eaten. Islam prohibits consumption of alcohol. Popular drinks are brewed coffee and sweetened tea that is steeped with cloves and cinnamon. Chewing of qat leaves that produce a mild intoxication is a common practice for both men and women.

Civil War: The brutality of the Siad Barre regime caused a civil war in the late 1980s. An estimated 50,000 to 60,000 civilians were murdered in northern Somalia alone in 1989-90. The army routinely bombed and shelled civilian areas believed to be sympathetic to the rebel causes. The army also laid land mines across wide areas, and destroyed water reservoirs and livestock. Nearly half a million refugees left the country to escape persecution by the Somali army. Due to the civil war and famine, hundreds of Somalis were dying. The international aid agencies organized convoys of supplies to be sent to the needy in the early 1990s, but organized gangs and bandits stole much of the relief supplies meant for the starving and dying people. Between 1991 and 1993 an estimated 250,000 to 300,000 Somalis died of the fighting or famine. In 1994 rival militia members signed a peace agreement under UN sponsorship, but the truce did not last long and fighting still continues.

Social Welfare: There is no official social welfare system, but people generally take care of their old and needy relatives. Some international agencies, such as CARE, have set up camps to train health workers and help farmers.

IMPORTANT DATES

1415—Ruler of Ifat state, Sa'd ad-Din, is killed and his army is destroyed.

1542—Muslim power is suppressed.

1854—Sir Richard Burton of England visits Somali coast.

1855—Somali spearmen attack Burton's camp.

1859—French buy the port of Obock from the Danakil clan of Somalia.

1869—Port of Assab is purchased by Italians.

1877—By a treaty, the British recognize Egyptian jurisdiction as far south as Ras Hafun.

1881—France sets up the Franco-Ethiopian Trading Company.

1884—Egyptians finally pull out from the Somali interior.

1891—The British and Italians agree to a treaty to define boundaries between their respective zones.

1894—Britain and Italy again agree to a treaty to define boundaries between their respective zones.

1899—A revolt is led by Muhammad ibn Abdullah Hasan, the "Mad Mullah."

1908—The boundary between Somalia and Ethiopia are confirmed by a treaty.

1910—The British withdraw to the coastal areas leaving interior to the *darwish,* followers of the imam.

1924—Italy receives the area west of the Jubba River.

1934—Ethiopia and Somalia clash over water wells along the border.

1941—British launch an offensive campaign against the Italian forces in Somalia.

1943—The first Somali political organization, the Somali Youth Club (SYC) is founded.

1944-45—A plague of locusts devastates the crops; thousands of livestock animals and camels die of starvation.

1946—District and Provincial Advisory Councils are created and elections are held.

1947—The SYC changes its name to Somali Youth League (SYL); its members number about 25,000.

1949-50—The UN gives administration of Somalia to Italy, UN Trust Territory of Somaliland is established.

1956—The SYL makes it illegal to name a political party after clan-families.

1960—Somalia becomes a free country as the British Somaliland and the Italian

Trust Territory of Somaliland are merged to form the Somali Republic; Somali National Bank is formed.

1961—A new constitution guarantees freedom of religion and also declares the Somali Republic an Islamic state.

1963—Somalia breaks diplomatic relations with the United Kingdom (resumes in 1968).

1964—A cease-fire is reached at the borders with Kenya and Ethiopia under the auspices of the Organization of African Unity (OAU).

1967—Mohamed Ibrahim Egal is nominated prime minister; Ali Shermarke is elected president.

1969—A political coup led by General Muhammed Siad Barre brings about many changes; the difference between Islam and socialism are made clear; the country's name is changed from Somali Republic to Somali Democratic Republic; the National Assembly is abolished; freedom of speech is limited; political parties are banned and the constitution is suspended; game reserves are set aside to protect native wildlife.

1970—Foreign banks and petroleum companies are nationalized.

1971—The government sets up a fishing cooperative, Somalfish; the government takes over the medical services.

1972—A new Somali script based on the Latin alphabet is introduced.

1973—Elementary school books are written and distributed in new Somali script.

1974—Somalia joins the Arab League.

1975—High school and higher education books in new Somali script are in use.

1975-76—Somalia suffers from one of the worst droughts in its history.

1977-78—Somali forces take over briefly the Ogaden region of Ethiopia which is inhabited almost entirely by ethnic Somalis.

1979—A new constitution is promulgated; the first elections to the People's Assembly are held.

1980—State of emergency is declared to curb political unrest.

1981—Somalia licences several Iraqi and Italian trawlers to fish the waters near Somalia; state of emergency is lifted.

1986—Diplomatic relations with Soviet Union are restored.

1988—Somalia concludes a nonaggression pact with Ethiopia.

1990—Siad Barre's bodyguards kill at least 65 people at a soccer match; 46 prominent Somalis were to be charged for calling for free elections, but the charges were later dropped; the United Somali Congress (USC) attacks Mogadishu; Siad Barre escapes and takes refuge in Nigeria.

1991—Somali National Movement (SNM) proclaims the "Republic of Somaliland" with capital at Hargeysa in the north on territory corresponding to the former British Somaliland; it receives no international recognition.

1992—UN Operation in Somalia (UNOSOM) begins to protect the food and other famine supplies by relief organizations (ends in March 1995); a Red Cross worker is fatally shot and wounded while distributing relief supplies; the UN mediates a truce between Muhammad Farah Aidid and Muhammad Ali Mahdi, two prominent warlords.

1993—A new president is elected; international troops arrive in Mogadishu; Aidid's forces kill 18 U.S. Rangers and at least 200 Somalis.

1994—The number of UN-sponsored military personnel in Somalia is estimated at 18,900; the U.S. mission in Somalia—Operation Restore Hope—ends when the last forces are pulled out of Somalia.

1995—Somali farmers have a good harvest after many years of drought; UN operations in Somalia end with the withdrawal of the remaining 2,400 peace-keeping troops; Aidid's forces seize Mogadishu Airport as UN troops pull back.

1996—Somalia joins several other African nations in not signing the Nuclear Arms Ban.

IMPORTANT PEOPLE

Colonel Ahmed Suleiman Abdulle, son-in-law of Siad Barre, ran the country with five other military officials after the coup of 1969

General Muhammad Farah Aidid, leader of the subclan Habir Gesdir; a powerful warlord and leader of the Somali National Alliance (SNA) in the early 1990s.

Sharif Abu Bakr bin Abdullah al-Aydarus (? -1503), founder of the Qadiriyyah sect in the Somali region.

Major General Jalle Muhammed Siad Barre (1921-1995), president from 1969 to 1991, leader of the bloodless political coup in 1969; became president and set up a Supreme Revolutionary Council (SRC), which he ruled like a dictator; was ousted in 1991 and went into exile to Nigeria.

Mohamed Ibrahim Egal, prime minister in 1967; a moderate politician who wanted to establish good relations with other African countries; also president of the breakaway "Republic of Somalia" in the north in 1991.

Sheik Muhammad Guled (? -1918), founder of the Salihiyyah sect in Somalia.

Muhammad ibn Abdullah Hasan (1860-1920), a national hero, religious leader, orator, poet, and imam of the puritanical Salihiyyah sect, who tried to get rid of all foreign influence that violated Islamic rules of behavior and called for Somali unity; his followers were called *darwish.*

Osman Ysuf Kenadid, inventor of the Osmaniya script that was used in forming country's first written literature.

Muhammad Ali Mahdi, head of the USC; became president in 1991; attended UN-sponsored peace talk in Nairobi with another warlord, Muhammad Farah Aidid.

Aden Abdullah Osman (1908-), nation's provisional president on the founding of Somalia, until Shermarke was elected; a respected national leader.

Abdirashid Ali Shermarke (1919-1969), first president of the Somali Republic; one of the founders of the Somali Youth League in 1943; a son of Osman Ysuf Kenadid; killed by his own bodyguard.

Sheik Ali Maye Durogba of Marka (? -1917), founder of the Ahmadiyyah sect in Somalia.

Abdullah Issa Muhammad (1921-), prime minister during the Italian Trusteeship Administration (1956~60); also served as Somali's first foreign minister.

Compiled by Chandrika Kaul, Ph.D.

INDEX

Page numbers that appear in boldface type indicate illustrations

About the Author

Mary Virginia Fox was graduated from Northwestern University and now lives near Madison, Wisconsin, conveniently located across the lake from the state capital and the University of Wisconsin. She is the author of forty-one books for young people and a score of feature articles for adult publications. For the Enchantment of the World series, she has also written about Papua New Guinea, Cyprus, Tunisia, Iran, New Zealand, and Bahrain.